CHILTERNS RAILWAYS
Remembered

Buckinghamshire, Bedfordshire & Hertfordshire

Leslie Oppitz

COUNTRYSIDE BOOKS

NEWBURY, BERKSHIRE

TO BARBARA

who went to Watford Grammar School
for Girls

Front cover shows Aylesbury Station c1910 (Lens of Sutton)

First Published 1991
© Leslie Oppitz 1991

COUNTRYSIDE BOOKS
3 Catherine Road
Newbury, Berkshire

ISBN 1 85306 163 8

Produced through MRM Associates Ltd., Reading
Typeset by Acorn Bookwork, Salisbury
Printed in England

Contents

ABBREVIATIONS

The following abbreviations are used on numerous occasions in this book:

A&BR	Aylesbury & Buckingham Railway
ASLEF	Associated Society of Locomotive Engineers and Firemen
B&CR	Bedford & Cambridge Railway
BR	British Rail
BTC	British Transport Commission
FOCAS	Friends of Cardington Airship Station
GCR	Great Central Railway
GNR	Great Northern Railway
GW&GC jt	Great Western & Great Central joint
GWR	Great Western Railway
LBLR	Leighton Buzzard Light Railway
HL&DR	Hertford, Luton & Dunstable Railway
IHPS	Iron Horse Preservation Society
L&BR	London & Birmingham Railway
LBSCR	London, Brighton & South Coast Railway
LCDR	London, Chatham & Dover Railway
LMS	London, Midland & Scottish Railway
LNER	London & North Eastern Railway
LNWR	London & North Western Railway
LPTB	London Passenger Transport Board
M&GC jt	Metropolitan & Great Central joint
MET	Metropolitan Railway
MR	Midland Railway
MS&LR	Manchester, Sheffield & Lincolnshire Railway
O&AT	Oxford & Aylesbury Tramroad
W&PRR	Watlington & Princes Risborough Railway
W&RR	Watford & Rickmansworth Railway
WH&BR	Ware, Hadham & Buntingford Railway

BIBLIOGRAPHY

In compiling Chilterns Railways Remembered, I have referred to numerous sources, many now out of print, which include the following and which can be recommended for further reading:

Author	Title	Publisher
R Davies and M D Grant	Forgotten Railways – Chilterns and Cotswolds	David & Charles
F G Cockman	The Railways of Hertfordshire	Hertfordshire Publications
F G Cockman	The Railway Age in Bedfordshire	The Bedfordshire Historical Record Society
Dennis Edwards and Ron Pigram	The Golden Years of the Metropolitan Railway and the Metroland Dream	Midas Books
Bill Simpson	The Banbury to Verney Junction Branch	Oxford Publishing Co
Bill Simpson	Oxford to Cambridge Railway Volume One: Oxford to Bletchley Volume Two: Bletchley to Cambridge	Oxford Publishing Co
Bill Simpson	The Aylesbury Railway	Oxford Publishing Co
R Lingard	Princes Risborough – Thame – Oxford Railway	Oxford Publishing Co
F W Goudie and Douglas Stuckey	West of Watford	Forge Books
C Baker	The Metropolitan Railway	The Oakwood Press
C T Goode	The Hertford Loop Line	The Oakwood Press
G & S Woodward	The Hatfield, Luton & Dunstable Railway (and on to Leighton Buzzard)	The Oakwood Press
Roger D Taylor and Brian Anderson	The Hatfield and St Albans Branch of the Great Northern Railway	The Oakwood Press
Ken Jones	The Wotton Tramway (Brill Branch)	The Oakwood Press
S A Leleux	The Leighton Buzzard Light Railway	The Oakwood Press
P Paye	The Buntingford Branch	The Oakwood Press

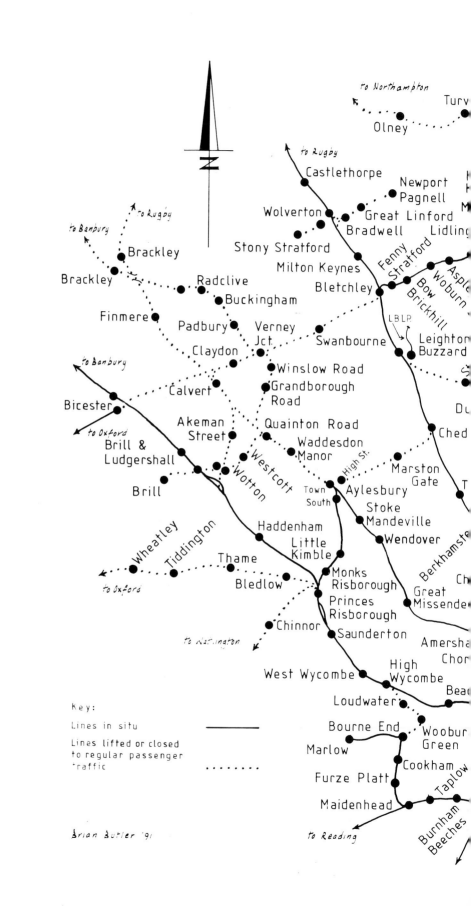

to Northampton

Turv[...]

Olney

to Rugby

Castlethorpe

Newport
Pagnell

Wolverton

Great Linford

Bradwell

Lidling[...]

Stony Stratford

to Rugby

to Banbury

Brackley

Brackley

Radclive

Buckingham

Milton Keynes

Fenny
Stratford

Bletchley

Aspl[...]

Woburn

Bow

Brickhill

Finmere

Padbury

Verney
Jct.

Swanbourne

LBLR

Leighton
Buzzard

Claydon

to Banbury

Winslow Road

Grandborough
Road

Bicester

Calvert

Akeman
Street

Quainton Road

Ched

to Oxford

Brill &
Ludgershall

Waddesdon
Manor

Marston
Gate

Du

Brill

Westcott

Wotton

High St.

Town
South

Aylesbury

T

Wheatley

Tiddington

Haddenham

Little
Kimble

Stoke
Mandeville

Wendover

Berkhamste[...]

Thame

Bledlow

Monks
Risborough

Great
Missende[...]

Ch

to Oxford

Chinnor

Princes
Risborough

to [Wat]ington

Saunderton

Amersha[...]

Chor

West Wycombe

High
Wycombe

Bea[...]

Loudwater

Key:

Lines in situ

Bourne End

Wooburn
Green

Lines lifted or closed
to regular passenger
traffic

Marlow

Cookham

Furze Platt

Taplow

Maidenhead

Burnham
Beeches

to Reading

Brian Butler '91

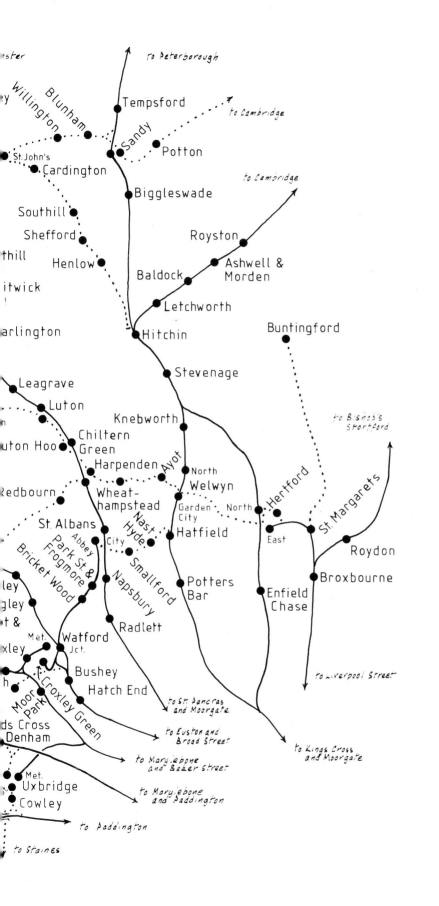

ACKNOWLEDGEMENTS

Acknowledgements go to the numerous libraries and record offices throughout Buckinghamshire, Bedfordshire and Hertfordshire and many of the surrounding areas, where staff have delved into records, to J L Smith of Lens of Sutton and to D K Jones and John H Meredith for their help in finding many old photographs.

The extract from a poem (Chapter 7) by the late Poet Laureate, Sir John Betjeman, is reproduced with the kind permission of John Murray (Publishers) Ltd.

Thanks also go to the following who generously contributed with information: Network Southeast (North); Roy B Miller, Curator, Buckinghamshire Railway Centre; Milton Keynes Museum of Industry & Rural Life; Douglas S Dunker; Bill Simpson; Graham Stroud, Marketing & PR Manager of the Leighton Buzzard Narrow Gauge Railway; Paul Adams of Friends of Cardington Airship Station; Roddy Dewe of Southill station; G Howe of Potton station; Peter van den Broek of Wotton; Danny Tyler of Westcott; Christopher Wilkinson of St Albans, London Road station; members of the Chinnor & Princes Risborough Railway Preservation Society.

Personal thanks go to Desmond Adams, Brian Butler and Vernon Deadman, to my wife, Joan, for her careful checking of the final manuscript and especially to David Nichols for all his help.

INTRODUCTION

Carriage doors slammed, a guard's whistle blew and a steam locomotive edged its way forward as a three coach passenger train slowly ground out of Quainton Road station. The locomotive was *Coventry no 1*, 0-6-0T locomotive no 24564, built to a Neilson Reid design at Hyde Park Works in 1939. One of the coaches was LNWR 1st class Diner no 77, one of a batch of twenty-five built at Wolverton between 1897 and 1901 and used frequently on the company's express trains. The coach was furnished to a high standard, similar to one that won the 'Grand-Prix' at the 1900 Paris Exhibition. Yet the train was not bound for Aylesbury or beyond but a run of under one mile along track owned by the Buckingham Railway Centre. The date was Sunday, 12th May 1991.

A visit to the above at Quainton Road can serve as a fascinating reminder of the many branch lines that once crossed the counties surrounding the Chiltern Hills. Many relics can still be found; old station buildings, engine sheds, road bridges or overgrown track-beds all go to make up what was once a network of branches throughout the area.

Conventional railways as known today began in the 1820s following George Stephenson's enthusiasm over locomotive engines. With the opening of the Stockton to Darlington Railway in 1825, the first steam train had arrived. In 1826 a line between Liverpool and Manchester was approved and three years later the famous Rainhill trials took place to establish which type of steam locomotive gave the best means of traction. Travelling was pretty uncomfortable in those early days with railway carriages beginning as stage-coach bodies attached to wagon bases. They were small, cramped and unlit and had no heating or travel facilities. When lighting came it was by oil lamps, subsequently to be replaced by gas lamps, and luxuries such as steam heating and comfortable seating came later in the century.

On 1st June 1834, the first major trunk railway to cut through the Chilterns was born when the first sod for the London & Birmingham Railway (L&BR) was cut at Chalk Farm. Work was soon to go ahead and, for three months from 20th July 1837, Boxmoor (today's Hemel Hempstead) was the railway's temporary terminus from the capital while Stephenson pressed northwards. Beyond Tring came the famous Tring Cutting through chalk, 2½ miles long and up to 60 ft deep. To complete the cutting, 1¾ million tons of material had to be removed taking 400 men over three years. On 17th September 1838 Birmingham was reached, providing Midlands industries with access to the markets they sought in London.

By the end of the century, no fewer than five major routes had penetrated the Chilterns. After the L&BR came the Great Northern Railway (GNR) empowered by an Act of June 1846 to build a railway from King's Cross to Doncaster and York. This reached Hitchin in 1850 and was in turn supplemented by the Midland Railway which reached Hitchin from Leicester in 1857. It was not long before the volume of traffic between Hitchin and King's Cross caused considerable congestion and in 1862 the GNR evicted Midland trains from its overcrowded King's Cross sidings. The Midland saw its only future was to build an independent route and this was completed in 1868 between Bedford and St Pancras via Luton and St Albans.

Meantime in 1854, the Wycombe Railway (with GWR backing) opened a line from Maidenhead to High Wycombe, to be followed in 1862 by an extension from High Wycombe to Thame via Princes Risborough. This became a main route to London for passengers travelling to London but when the Great Western & Great Central joint line opened in 1906, traffic quickly diverted to Marylebone and Paddington on a shorter and more direct journey.

A fifth route through the Chilterns reached Rickmansworth in 1887 when the Metropolitan Railway built outwards from Baker Street. Chesham was reached in 1889 and Aylesbury in 1892 where it met existing Aylesbury & Buckinghamshire Railway tracks. In 1899 the Great Central Railway (GCR) opened a line between Rugby and Quainton Road as part of a bid by chairman, Sir Edward Watkin, to link the North and Midlands with London – and eventually beyond to Paris. To reach London the GCR had to use Metropolitan Railway tracks, but the ambitious GCR sought an improved route with straighter track and lesser gradients, so a link was opened in 1905 south of Calvert (between Grendon Underwood junction and Ashendon junction) carrying trains across to the Princes Risborough–High Wycombe line.

From these major routes, branch lines developed where steam trains made their way across open stretches of countryside, linking remote villages and towns. In numerous instances passenger traffic remained light throughout, although goods traffic provided an essential service to many agricultural areas. Some lines suffered an early demise simply because they became uneconomic but, with road transport fast competing, the Beeching cuts of the early 1960s also took their toll.

This book intends to examine not only the lives of these lines in the counties of Buckinghamshire, Bedfordshire and Hertfordshire, their growth, decline and closure, but also the preserved lines and societies of today that are dedicated to keep the past alive. It also provides the reader with a means to explore 'lost' stations that can be found and the numerous trackbeds that have survived, many converted to footpaths.

Chapter 1

'LORD EBURY'S LINE'

(Watford to Rickmansworth)

'When Watford is joined to Uxbridge and the Great Western, it will be possible to bring smokeless Welsh coal to the Chess and Colne valleys', claimed Lord Ebury at the ceremony of 'turning the first sod' of the Watford & Rickmansworth Railway (W&RR) on 22nd November 1860. But lack of finance plus opposition from Uxbridge landowners meant that his dream never materialised and what transpired was a 4½ mile single track railway from Watford to Rickmansworth. Lord Ebury was born Robert Grosvenor, the third and youngest son of the Marquis of Westminster. He served as MP for Middlesex and when he became Baron Ebury he acquired the well known Moor Park estate. It was from here that his plans to link Uxbridge with Watford were shaped, a proposal which would have also usefully provided a link between the West and lines to the Midlands and the North thus avoiding London.

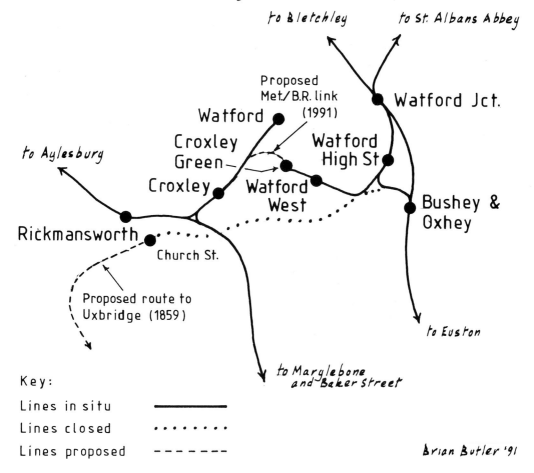

Closure of the Rickmansworth branch passed relatively uneventfully on 2nd March 1952 with only a handful of enthusiasts on the last train. Here earlier the same day an Oerlikon set awaits departure to Watford. (John H. Meredith)

The ceremony of turning the first sod took place at Tolpits Farm on a warm and pleasant November day, close to what later became the Moor Lane level crossing. The invited guests assembled at Moor Park from where they were directed to the site by flags. At the sound of a bugle, places were taken and Lord Ebury proceeded. After a blessing given by the vicar of Rickmansworth, there were three cheers for the Queen, the National Anthem was played and then three cheers for Lord Ebury and to the success of the line. The party plus the band then proceeded to the National School Rooms at Rickmansworth to the strains of 'Oh, the Roast Beef of Old England'.

The railway's formal opening on 1st October 1862 was quite different and there was virtually no celebration although when the first train arrived at Rickmansworth hundreds of people welcomed it. The town's original station was a basic wooden construction reported to be 'flimsy and leaky'. Just beyond the station, trains crossed the Grand Union Canal. The W&RR Act decreed that the bridge should be 'good and substantial' and 'with a soffit at least 10 feet over the top water level'. Initially the branch carried six trains each way daily and the only intermediate station was at the southern end of Watford High Street. Yet the push-pull two-coach trains hauled by an 0-6-2 freight tank locomotive were busy for both passengers and goods.

The W&RR was operated from the outset by the LNWR which paid the independent company 'a sum equal to 50% of the amount of the gross earnings from tolls, rates etc ...' until the LNWR took over the line completely on 27th June 1881. In addition to the considerable sidings traffic on the branch, the carriage of watercress developed and it became a common sight to see hampers being transported to the market at Watford and stock used on the branch acquired the nickname 'watercress trains'.

Schemes to electrify LNWR lines were considered in 1907 but it was not until four years later that definite proposals were put forward. Even so it was to be many more years before electric services reached the branch. In November 1911 the LNWR took over the running of the North London Railway and plans followed for a new branch to be opened between Watford and Croxley Green. A steam passenger service commenced on 15th June 1912 with freight traffic starting on 1st October. Trains left the Rickmansworth line at Croxley Green junction with part of the branch doubled for the extra traffic. During February 1913, track was laid from Bushey & Oxhey station joining the W&RR just south of Watford High Street station (known as the 'new line') and another loop, forming a triangle, allowed steam trains from Euston to run directly to Croxley Green. On 10th March 1913 Croxley Green station was totally destroyed by a fire said to have been started deliberately by suffragettes.

Electric trains reached Watford from Euston on 10th July 1922 and the electric service to Croxley Green started on 30th October 1922. Rickmansworth's wooden station was replaced by a brick building but passengers at the terminus had to wait until 26th September 1927 for an electric service, by which time it had become a London, Midland & Scottish Railway (LMS) branch. Full-sized cars on the Croxley Green and Rickmansworth branches were found to put an excessive load on the local electricity sub-station, but these were replaced by nine coaches from ex-LNWR/London Electric Railway tube stock when these were withdrawn from the Euston–Watford route in 1930/31. When Watford Football Club was playing at home extra coaches were often added. On 4th December 1982, a new station, known as Watford Stadium Halt was opened to serve supporters. The then chairman of the Watford Football Club, Elton John, and Lord Aberdare, chairman of the Football Trust, performed the ceremony.

During the 1920s competition from bus services made itself felt. In 1921 the Rickmansworth & District Omnibus Company began

LNWR locomotives at Watford Junction station c1919. The leading engine is 2-4-0 no. 193 'Rocket', a Precedent class locomotive built about 1890. The second is 4-4-0 no 1957 rebuilt as a 2 cylinder Renown class 2P. (D K Jones)

operating services to Watford and, although the company did not last, it was soon replaced by the National Omnibus & Transport Company which extended its services from Croxley Green to Rickmansworth in 1924. The Lewis Omnibus Company followed, operating from Rickmansworth to Watford and St Albans. This company also took over the Metropolitan (MET) bus service (see chapter 7) from Watford MET station to the town centre. There were further problems when the MET reached Watford from its Rickmansworth station in 1925. When a public passenger service began on November 2nd, 35 electric trains daily were reaching Baker Street (and Aldgate in peak hours) plus the same number of steam trains to and from Marylebone. The LMS considered the MET branch plans superfluous but the MET countered saying that the LMS Croxley Green station was at least half a mile from

Watford High Street station in LNWR days c1910. The station opened on 1st October 1862 with six trains on the Rickmansworth branch each way daily. (Lens of Sutton)

the village and serving nobody. It claimed that it stood like 'a pelican in the wilderness'.

The nine tube coaches introduced in 1930/31 were replaced in 1939 by spare main line stock. These were Oerlikon saloon car sets, already twenty years old, which lasted on the Rickmansworth branch until its closure in 1952. A lady who travelled in these coaches in the late 1940s when a pupil at Watford Grammar School for Girls tells of how she and her friends used to collect caterpillars on the way to the station and then race them along the compartment seats during the journey. Unfortunately for the girls the practice was reported to the headmistress and there followed a public ticking off during school assembly!

The last train from Rickmansworth (renamed Rickmansworth Church Street in September 1950) ran on March 2nd 1952. As the 10.45 pm to Watford made its final run, only a dozen or so railway enthusiasts were carried plus one 'bona fide' passenger. The 'right away' was given and the lights of 'Ricky' were quickly left behind. Crossing the canal, the train gathered speed up to Tolpits Farm, passed Brightwells Farm and then rattled down to Croxley Green junction, pausing for the staff to be handed up to the box for the last time from a passenger train. One bereaved enthusiast re-marked, 'It was a quiet funeral'.

The track lasted another 15 years with the occasional goods train working the spur down to Dickinson's Croxley Mills or possibly shunting in the Universal Asbestos factory sidings. At Brightwells Farm another siding led to the Colne Valley Water Company's sidings where a 2 ft gauge light railway was built in 1932. Not far from Watford High Street station another siding served Benskins Brewery with tracks reaching its four-storeyed malthouse plus a short spur to the boiler and brewhouse. The last rail despatch of beer left in 1953 although barley was delivered by rail until 1956. Freight services on the Rickmansworth branch lasted until 2nd January 1967 when the line closed completely.

The Oerlikons survived on the Croxley Green branch until April 1960. When visited in May 1991, smart class 313 dual-voltage sets

Watford High Street station on 3rd May 1991. The building beyond the awning was demolished to make way for a road link. (Author)

15

The LNWR Croxley Green station, seen here c1910, was at one time a grand affair. In March 1913 the station and buildings were totally destroyed by a fire started by suffragettes. (Lens of Sutton)

Croxley Green station today comprises a temporary platform and there is only a Monday to Friday peak service. Perhaps one day the MET line from Rickmansworth will join the branch to give MET trains a through run to Watford Junction? (Author)

operated the three morning and evening peak trains still running on the branch which since January 1991 has otherwise been closed. A 'temporary' platform has replaced the original Croxley Green station, where derelict buildings were finally demolished in late 1989. One wonders how much longer the branch can last, especially since a recent survey found trains were carrying an average of only ten passengers!

Perhaps all is not lost. The London Underground is considering an ambitious scheme costing around £15 million to link the MET line with BR's Croxley Green branch in a link-up achieved by the construction of a new S-shaped viaduct across Watford Road near Cassiobridge, Croxley Green. This would allow MET travellers from Baker Street direct travel to Watford High Street and Junction stations. Funding, says the Underground report, would be privately sought by development of land, probably for housing, which could be freed by the closure of Watford MET station. Perhaps the MET's attempts to reach Watford town centre in 1927 may yet succeed, seventy years on!

Chapter 2

BROAD GAUGE TO HIGH WYCOMBE

(Bourne End to High Wycombe)

Had early planners had their way then a railway might well have linked the former Bourne End–High Wycombe branch which opened in 1854 with the Great Western Railway (GWR) Uxbridge (High Street) branch. The line would have left the Bourne End branch just south of Loudwater station and then passed through Beaconsfield, Chalfont St Peter and Denham. A Bill was drawn up in 1864 but nothing further developed. Later in 1898 an idea came from the Marlow & Henley Railway Company (promoted by the GWR) to link the terminus at Henley-on-Thames with Marlow. Again the proposal did not proceed but had both these plans come about then tracks would have existed direct from Henley across to Uxbridge, thus increasing the rather sparse GWR suburban network around London.

The Wycombe Railway was incorporated on 27th July 1846 initially to build a railway from Maidenhead to High Wycombe. This was a single-track broad gauge line, worked from the outset by the GWR. The opening of the line was delayed for a number of years, partly because of financial difficulties and the bankruptcy of its contractor but despite setbacks, services began on 1st August 1854. Maidenhead station is now known as Taplow, and the original intermediate stations were Maidenhead (Wycombe Branch), Cookham, Marlow Road (renamed Bourne End in 1874), Wooburn Green (spelt Woburn Green until October 1872) and

Bourne End station before closure to passengers of the Bourne End–High Wycombe section. This picture, taken in the 1960s, shows the line to Maidenhead off to the left and the Marlow branch to the right. Through trains from Maidenhead to Marlow need to reverse. (Lens of Sutton)

Loudwater. Maidenhead (Wycombe Branch) station, situated close to an overbridge where the Great West Road crossed the track, has today disappeared beyond all trace.

Under an Act of 17th August 1857, the Wycombe Railway obtained powers to extend to Princes Risborough and a later Act agreed extensions to Oxford and Aylesbury (see chapter 3). With these extensions completed by the mid-1860s, the High Wycombe to Maidenhead branch became the principal route to London for passengers in the High Wycombe and Princes Risborough areas. All Wycombe Railway lines were worked by the GWR and the company's independent existence, owning over 44 miles of broad gauge track, ended on 1st February 1867 when it was absorbed by the GWR. Some three years later the Bourne End to High Wycombe branch was converted to standard gauge track.

The railway reached Marlow in 1873. A short branch from Marlow Road to Marlow was opened on 28th June of that year by the Great Marlow Railway Company. This was also a single line and it was worked by electric train token, being the first GWR branch to use this system. On 1st January 1874 it was decided to change the name of Marlow Road station to Bourne End, thus avoiding any confusion. This short branch was to prosper and the train service became affectionately known as the 'Marlow Donkey'. Like the Wycombe Railway, it was worked by the GWR from the start although it did not amalgamate with the larger company until 1st July 1897.

Marlow has been described as 'the happiest town in Bucks'. In the centre, narrow streets converge on the Market Place where the old Town Hall once stood – now the Crown Hotel. A stone obelisk stands nearby, erected in 1822 by the trustees of the Reading and Hatfield Turnpike Trust. During its life the trust improved the road so that the journey to the spa at Bath was shortened and the route became known as Gout Road! West Street today, with its almost unbroken line of houses of charm and interest, is a part of this route.

Bourne End station, May 1991, where the former bay platform for Marlow has been given over to light industry. Much of the trackbed to High Wycombe survives as a public footpath but part has been consumed by the M40 motorway. (Author)

In 1906 the Great Western & Great Central joint (GW & GC jt) opened a line to London via Beaconsfield which provided a more direct access to the capital, taking just over 6 miles off the earlier route via Bourne End and Maidenhead. Passengers were quick to transfer to the line and Bourne End branch suffered considerably. It survived the earlier Beeching cuts but, as traffic continued to fall, closure of part of the route became inevitable. In 1972 British Rail told local councillors, 'Increase passenger receipts or the line will die'. The result was the formation of the Marlow/Maidenhead Railway Passengers' Association which has so far proved successful in saving the Marlow branch. The Bourne End to High Wycombe section suffered when closure to passengers came on 4th May 1970, leaving Bourne End as a junction where Maidenhead trains would reverse back to Marlow.

Before this partial closure, there were frequent diversions along the branch and larger 4-6-0 and 2-8-0 locomotives could be seen, but trains were normally hauled by GWR class 14XX 0-4-2Ts with around 20 each way daily, some dividing at Bourne End. On 15th July 1973 Great Western Society locomotives were steamed to commemorate the 100 years since trains had first reached Marlow. Two weeks later on 29th July ex-LBSCR class H2 no 32425 *Trevose Head* hauled an excursion train from BR's Southern Region over the line to Marlow from High Wycombe to return via Bourne End and Maidenhead.

Today there are still over twenty trains daily on weekdays but, with the Bourne End to High Wycombe section gone, reversal is necessary at Bourne End to reach Marlow. Trains run hourly on Saturdays and Sundays in the summer. Both platforms are used at Bourne End for occasional shuttle services with railcar trailer

Ex-GWR 2-6-2T class 6100 (introduced in 1931 and designed by C B Collett) pulls into Wooburn Green station probably early 1950s. (Lens of Sutton)

Parcels await collection at Loudwater in the 1960s. During the latter part of the last century this branch carried through London trains from the High Wycombe and Princes Risborough areas. This lasted until 1906 when a more direct route via Beaconsfield was opened. (Lens of Sutton)

Marlow's original station plus its four sidings and goods shed have long since gone. The branch opened in June 1873 and the train, still available today, became affectionately known as the 'Marlow Donkey'. (Lens of Sutton)

combinations having to grind sharply round a curved connection onto the Marlow branch. This section gives excellent views of the river Thames and the Berkshire hills beyond, leading to a single platform unstaffed halt at the terminus. Gone is the original station with its four goods sidings and an engine shed. There was also once a timber yard with its own siding but this was disconnected in July 1970 when freight traffic on the branch came to an end.

Bourne End station still retains some of the typically GWR prestige. The former line northwards continued its journey up the valley of the river Wye with the Chilterns rising to a tree-clad ridge to the left and pleasing Buckinghamshire uplands to the right stretching towards Beaconsfield. This valley was once the centre of a paper industry with mill-boards made near Bourne End and,

Marlow's single-platform station today has a pleasing appearance and is conveniently placed for the town. There had earlier been threats the branch might close but, thanks to the efforts of the Marlow/ Maidenhead Railway Passengers' Association, it has survived. (Author)

towards Wooburn Green, sidings served paper works. Onward the line followed the sweep of the Chiltern ridge to Loudwater, the home of Ford's blotting paper. It is from Loudwater that the traveller first caught sight of the GW & GC jt line high up on the adjacent hillside which the branch train would shortly join on its ascent towards High Wycombe.

Much of the trackbed survives with sections converted to a public footpath, yet the trains are over 20 years gone. At Wooburn Green only the trackbed can be found whilst at Loudwater the station site today comprises industrial units. Part of the line has been consumed by the forever busy M40 motorway, with its sliproads and roundabouts connecting with the A40. Truly in this area the motorcar has visibly ousted the railway.

Chapter 3

GWR LINES FROM PRINCES RISBOROUGH

(Princes Risborough to Oxford and Princes Risborough to Watlington)

Princes Risborough to Oxford

In September 1859, Edward Griffin of Towersey Manor, filled a wheelbarrow, walked along a plank amid three resounding cheers and emptied the contents some little way off. Other directors performed the same task, an operation which was followed by dinner and speeches at Mr Griffin's house. The ceremony of 'cutting the first sod' for the Wycombe Railway's proposed line from High Wycombe to Thame had been completed. Yet the start was purely a notional one since much had to be done. A meeting was held at Thame's Spread Eagle Hotel and it was announced that £40,000 would be required. After much persuasion from the promoters, sufficient capital was eventually forthcoming.

Earlier numerous lines had been proposed for the area. In 1836 there were plans for a 'railroad' from Cheltenham to Tring via Thame and Aylesbury. This had the backing of the London & Birmingham Railway seeking a shorter route to the capital but, despite strong attempts to get it through Parliament, the plan failed. Another plan came from the LNWR in 1852 for a line from north of Oxford through Thame and Beaconsfield to Hounslow but again the idea failed. Eventually, on 28th June 1861, Parliament agreed that the Wycombe Railway could extend from Princes Risborough to Oxford as well as to Aylesbury on broad gauge.

Bledlow station had a single platform face only yet it included a signal box, a level crossing, a 2 ton crane and a siding. When it opened in 1862 there were four trains each way daily. (Lens of Sutton)

Thame was reached on 1st August 1862 although there was no official ceremony. During the afternoon a party of directors and shareholders travelled the line from Wycombe to Thame in three coaches hauled by a 'Sun' class 2-2-2 locomotive named *Sunbeam* with 6 ft diameter driving wheels. A regular service from Paddington to Thame began the following day with four trains each way daily via Maidenhead taking around 2¾ hours. The single fares were 9/– (45p), 6/3d (31½p) and 4/– (20p) for first, second and third class respectively. There was an intermediate station at Bledlow and a halt at Towersey.

The line was welcomed by the people of Thame, one of its benefits being a reduction in the price of coal. The line was broad gauge, worked by the GWR from the start and was also the first to use the train staff and ticket system. Work quickly began on the Thame to Oxford section with considerable earthworks required for the construction of Horspath Tunnel nearer the Oxford end of the line. In all, approximately 640,000 cubic yards of blue clay had to be dug out and the tunnel, 1,584 feet in length, had to be lined throughout.

In his book, *Princes Risborough – Thame – Oxford Railway*, Richard Lingard wrote of the navvies who built the line. There were no recorded incidents of bad behaviour yet they obviously liked their drink. The men often called at 'The King and Queen' at Wheatley where they collected buckets of spirits on yokes. The vicar of Wheatley, the Reverend Elton, regularly visited the men at work and it seemed his preaching had some success for many would attend the 'entertainment' provided in the evenings in the local schoolroom. The vicar supported the building of the railway on religious grounds saying he was sure it would have 'a beneficial influence in raising the character of the people'!

The extension to Kennington junction, south of Oxford, opened on 24th October 1864. There were intermediate stations at Tiddington, Wheatley, Morris Cowley and Littlemore plus Horspath Halt near the tunnel. After less than a month the line carried a

Chinnor station, c1910. This was the Watlington branch's main intermediate station with a goods yard and sidings. (Lens of Sutton)

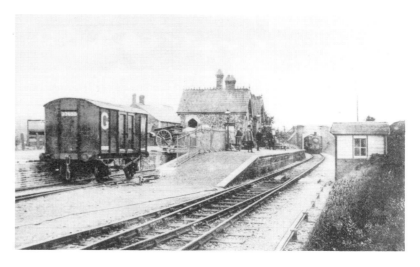

Royal visitor. On Monday, 21st November, the Prince of Wales plus numerous other dignitaries travelled on the 10.40 am train from London to Thame for a meet of the Earl of Macclesfield's hounds at the 'Three Pigeons' at Milton Common. The party returned by the 2.55 pm train.

The original station at Princes Risborough comprised two short platforms and wooden buildings. The town later had a four-line station with bays at the northern ends of the up and down platforms. Thame station had a wooden all-over roof covering the two platforms and a large goods yard with four sidings on the up side. The branch's broad gauge did not last for long. On 1st February 1867 the Wycombe Railway amalgamated with the Great Western Railway and on 23rd August 1870 the entire line from High Wycombe to Kennington junction closed for conversion to narrow (or standard) gauge. Just over a week later passenger services resumed with goods traffic following after a few days.

There were complaints that services were inadequate and in 1893 an additional early train was added in each direction. This was still thought insufficient and competition came from a local company which ran a bus twice daily to Aylesbury to catch LNWR trains. The connection gave a longer day in town plus a cheaper overall fare. In 1906 the new Great Western & Great Central joint (GW & GC jt) line from High Wycombe to Paddington opened reducing the journey time to 1½ hours.

By the 1930s passenger traffic was steadily declining and as an economy measure railmotors were introduced between Princes Risborough and Thame. During the Second World War an American Military Hospital was established near Wheatley which meant hospital trains arrived from the East coast ports often pulled by unfamiliar Great Eastern Railway B12s and D16s. There were times too when the Reading line was obstructed by bombing and expresses for Worcester used the Thame route. The blackout caused problems and it was not unknown for passengers to get out of a train when it stopped between stations. In 1941, with many

Aston Rowant not long before closure. Beyond the station the single track passed under the main London to Oxford A40 road. The varying gradient can be seen giving the branch its 'switch-back' nature. (Lens of Sutton)

men serving in the forces, women staff were taken on. As the war progressed, their hours became longer and eventually they carried out the same duties as the men. A woman guard recalled seeing sparks flying out of a locomotive's chimney and, giving it little thought, she later discovered that she had been in charge of an ammunition train!

After the war passenger traffic fell and rumours of closure circulated. On 23rd October 1959 the British Transport Commission (BTC) officially denied the possibility but said that the matter was 'under investigation' – so often a first step to closure. By 1962 the threat was real enough. The BTC reckoned the line was losing £26,000 a year and that at times only a handful of passengers were using it. Finally, after much local indignation, it was announced that passenger services would be withdrawn as from 7th January 1963. The last train comprised five coaches instead of the usual two, hauled by 2-6-2 Prairie tank no 6111. As it left Oxford a nearby diesel gave a farewell salute from its horn. Wheatley's passengers joining the train included a man dressed in deep mourning complete with frock coat and top hat while another dressed as Dr Beeching. Crowds turned out at the various intermediate stations and at Princes Risborough the relief stationmaster, R W Cox, honoured the occasion by wearing his GWR stationmaster's hat. The train pulled out on its return to Oxford to the strains of 'Land of Hope and Glory' and finally 'Auld Lang Syne'.

Sections of the track exist today. Since closure freight trains have served Morris Cowley from the Oxford end, and oil traffic has reached Thame from Princes Risborough. Thame station has disappeared with only two platform edges remaining.

Princes Risborough to Watlington

The villagers of Watlington have the Earl of Macclesfield, squire of nearby Shirburn Castle, to thank for their branch to Princes Risborough. It was through his persistence, and later his involvement as a director, that in 1869, the independent Watlington &

Princes Risborough Railway (W&PRR) Company's Act was passed. Earlier an Act of 1864 had agreed the Wallingford & Watlington Railway but only the portion from Cholsey (then Wallingford Road) to Wallingford was built, opening in 1866. Had it been completed, a through route from the Bristol main line to the Wycombe Railway would have been created. The failure of the scheme much displeased Watlington's residents, including the Earl of Macclesfield.

Work on the Watlington to Princes Risborough branch proceeded at low cost since there was little heavy engineering involved. The standard gauge line, which ran southwest from Princes Risborough along the Chilterns foothills, opened on 15th August 1872 with a service of three trains each way daily. There were two intermediate stations at Chinnor and Aston Rowant. The company had given an undertaking to the Board of Trade that the single line would be worked on the staff and ticket system but initially, and since traffic was very light, only one engine in steam working was employed.

Because of the low number of passengers, the independent company soon ran into financial difficulties. The original Princes Risborough station was a small wooden platform just short of the GWR station, so passengers had to walk to change trains, although a goods connection existed. Locomotives and rolling stock were hired from the GWR and it was not long before the independent company's debts could not be paid. An approach was made to the GWR to work the line at an annual rent of £600 but it was refused. The GWR claimed that special locomotives would be required over a branch so lightly constructed – a typical ploy used to run down a line until it could be cheaply acquired. Eventually the GWR obtained powers to purchase the W&PRR by an Act of 1883

A GWR 0-6-0T Pannier tank no 1969 waits at Watlington on 30th July 1949. This locomotive was built at Wolverhampton 1889/1890 as a saddle tank and was rebuilt as a pannier in the 1920s or 1930s. (John H Meredith)

at about half the cost it had taken to build the line. Formal transfer took place on 1st June of that year with actual possession going ahead on 31st December.

The GWR showed little interest in improving its newly acquired line. £3,750 was authorised to put it into proper order but nothing much was done. Trackside fencing was occasionally improved but not to a good enough standard for a farmer at Lewknor who demanded a fence high enough to stop his turkeys flying over it! The GWR took over two tank engines and one of these, a 2-4-0 side-tank, received the number 1384 and was rebuilt at Swindon in 1899. After working other GWR branches it passed into the hands of Colonel Stephens for service on the Weston, Clevedon & Portishead Railway. When the locomotive acquired the name *Hesperus*, it was suggested (R K Kirkland, *The Railway Magazine*, June 1956) that it was given this name because of some of the wreck-like locomotives on the Colonel's railways!

In May 1890 the GWR obtained clearance from the Board of Trade to cancel the undertaking (given to the W&PRR and never

The terminus at Watlington in the 1960s. This station opened in August 1872 with a service of three trains each way daily. Earlier plans to link Watlington with Wallingford never materialised. (Lens of Sutton)

Watlington station site (on strictly private land) nearly 35 years after closure. The proud days of the GWR and the 'Watlington Flyer' are long since past. (Author)

There are hopes that the Chinnor & Princes Risborough Railway Preservation Society will soon be providing a passenger service. Rolling stock was being gathered when visited in May 1991 and this low-loader (minus its load) was pushed by 25 tough enthusiasts from Thame to Chinnor raising over £1000! (Author)

carried out) to work a staff and ticket system thus avoiding the need to install an expensive block telegraph. Permission was granted in September 1906 to introduce steam railcars and, at the same time to encourage local passenger traffic, rail-level halts were opened at Bledlow Bridge, Kingston Crossing and Lewknor Bridge. The halt at Bledlow Bridge was an improvement for the local folk since the earlier Bledlow station on the Oxford line was a mile from the village. As railcars disappeared from GWR stock, ordinary train working resumed and in September 1925 an additional halt was opened at Wainhill Crossing.

Leaving Princes Risborough, the Watlington and Oxford single-track branches ran side-by-side for about half a mile and it was said that timetables were arranged so that trains could not race each other on the two routes. The principal intermediate station was Chinnor with its buildings on the up-side, a goods yard and sidings. The platform was often attractively adorned with flowers. On the down side, several sidings laid in 1927 served a large lime and cement works and this track still exists. A succession of changing gradients followed giving the branch a switch-back character. Beyond the rather isolated station of Aston Rowant the line passed under the main London–Oxford road before reaching the terminus. Watlington station, close to Shirburn Castle but about a mile from the town, had only a single short platform. There was a run-round loop, a goods yard with three sidings and a locomotive shed.

It was inevitable that such a lightly-used line should fall victim to the 'Beeching Axe' despite the many protests of its loyal users. The last journey took place on Saturday, 29th June 1957, when, after 85 years of faithful service, the branch was closed to passengers. Because so many gathered for the event, an extra coach was added but, when the train arrived at Chinnor, this was hardly adequate. The *Thame Gazette* reported, 'After a reasonably good imitation of a rugger scrum, the Parish Council, principal inhabitants and freight were thrust aboard by unseen forces from the rear and the journey commenced.' A notice on the side of the train read, 'Well done, thou good and faithful servant, enter thou into the joy of the overlords'. Watlington station buildings (on strictly private land) survive in a sorry state. The proud days of the GWR and the 'Watlington Flyer' have unhappily long since gone.

Yet there is hope that passenger trains may once again run along part of the track. The Chinnor & Princes Risborough Railway Preservation Society has already made good progress towards providing such a service. With the use of a Baguley 0-4-0 diesel (built for Double Diamond in 1952) plus three coaches, a wagon and a crane, use has already been made of the existing stretch of track between Princes Risborough and the Chinnor Cement Works. This stretch was disconnected from BR's tracks on 18th May 1991 and the society is hopeful that passenger trains can commence by 1993 or 1994. At Princes Risborough the existing island platform plus the station's signal box will be used. Another signal box has been acquired from Gerrards Cross, but when seen by the author it was 'in bits' at Chinnor awaiting assembly. It is expected that trains will eventually reach Aston Rowant.

The preservation society recently gained a useful contribution to its funds when a low wagon had to be collected from Thame. Twenty five tough enthusiasts pushed the truck first to Princes Risborough, then back to Chinnor – a distance of nine miles. Including stops, it took them five hours – but they raised over £1,000!

Chapter 4

CROSS COUNTRY ROUTES

(Bletchley/Verney Junction/Banbury and Verney Junction/Oxford)

Bletchley station on the former London & Birmingham line which was completed in July 1837. When a branch from Bletchley to Banbury was opened by the Buckingham Railway on 1st May 1850, there were great celebrations in the town. (Lens of Sutton)

The line between Bletchley and Banbury (Merton Street) enjoyed many Royal connections. Stowe, with its splendid park and mansion built for the Dukes of Buckingham during the 17th and 18th centuries, attracted numerous visitors and many arrived by train. In 1881 the third and last Duke of Buckingham returned by rail from service in India to receive a civic welcome and there were further celebrations four years later when crowds welcomed the Duke's return at the station after his marriage. More recently, Royal visits have included the arrival of the late King George VI and Queen Elizabeth plus other members of the Royal family in May 1950 on their way to Silverstone and in April 1966 the present Queen and the Duke of Edinburgh arrived by Royal Train (after the line had been closed to passenger traffic) with the train stabled overnight at Padbury.

The small market town of Buckingham with its Georgian Town Hall was unfortunate since, during the earlier days of 'railway mania', it was overlooked by the main railway companies and transport facilities remained poor. It is recorded that in the late 18th century a coach service had run from Banbury on alternate

days calling at Buckingham and Winslow on its way to Holborn. A branch of the Grand Union Canal reached the town in 1801 but it was many more years before the railways arrived. When the London & Birmingham Railway (L&BR) completed its line in September 1838, Buckingham was bypassed, with Tring becoming the nearest station. In 1844 the Great Western Railway (GWR) opened a broad-gauge branch from Didcot to Oxford with plans to continue to Rugby. Each saw the other as a threat to its future and many skirmishes followed. It was L&BR's amalgamation with the Grand Junction Railway and the Manchester & Birmingham Railway in 1846 to form the London & North Western Railway (LNWR), plus the Gauge Commission's recommendations largely against broad gauge, that went towards resolving the problems.

It was mainly thanks to the efforts of the Duke of Buckingham and Sir Harry Verney that the Buckingham Railway came about. With a wide area of the county still without railway communication, bills were passed by Parliament, although the lines as originally authorised did not materialise. The proposals included a line from Harrow to Aylesbury but this was dropped, with part of the route later completed by the Aylesbury & Buckingham Railway. When finally built, the Buckingham Railway consisted of a line from Bletchley to Banbury and another from Verney Junction to Oxford. It was decided that the railway to Banbury should receive priority, yet at 5 pm on 20th April 1847 near the Cross Keys public house, in the Landborough Road at Buckingham, the ceremony of 'cutting the first turf' passed almost unnoticed. The same could not be said for the events that were to follow. In a very short time the

Class 2F LMS 0-6-0 no 3195 seen at Bletchley on 19th April 1930. Initially known as a 1798 class locomotive, it was built at Derby in 1888 to designs of S W Johnson. (D K Jones)

31

Winslow station shortly before closure to passengers on 1st January 1968. Before Verney Junction opened in 1868, this was an important point for changing trains between the Banbury and Oxford routes. (Lens of Sutton)

Winslow station building in May 1991 was in a derelict state. Despite this, a number of Milton Keynes shopping specials left the station in November 1990 and there are also hopes that one day a service may be reinstated between Bicester, Bletchley and Bedford. (Author)

construction sites around the sleepy county town became a 'hard drinking and riotous centre' – so much so that the directors had to bring in a full time chaplain and several scripture readers in an attempt to calm things down!

Construction between Bletchley and Banbury took just under three years. There were periods of financial difficulty and instead of the double track intended, single track was built. Four trains ran each way daily, worked by the LNWR. When the line opened to passengers on 1st May 1850 there were great celebrations with many people at Banbury to watch the 6.30 am train depart. The station was gaily decorated with flags, there were booths and stalls and, throughout the day, a brass band played. There was even greater excitement when the railway telegraph brought news of the birth of the Duke of Connaught, third son of Queen Victoria. Later that year, on 1st October, the line to Oxford opened as far as Islip, extended to a temporary station at Oxford Road on 2nd December and on 20th May 1851 opened throughout. The opportunity was immediately seized to run excursions to the Great

Claydon station in the 1960s on the line from Verney Junction to Bicester. Freight traffic came to an end in January 1964 and passenger services closed in January 1968. (Lens of Sutton)

Exhibition in London's Hyde Park and when a special train left Oxford on 21st May, there were ten coaches carrying some 400 passengers.

Travelling the line from Bletchley, the first intermediate station on the line towards Verney Junction was Swanbourne although the village was over a mile away. Despite its remoteness, the station at its peak boasted takings averaging £400 a week. Swanbourne's remoteness was challenged in British Rail's 1955 modernisation programme. There were plans to build two large marshalling yards – one at Carlisle and the other near Swanbourne station. The proposal included the building of a vast concrete flyover at Bletchley to connect the main line with the Oxford line and also link the Oxford line with the Cambridge line without involving Bletchley station. The cost was put at £1.6 million. Work on the flyover began in September 1958 and involved the necessary compulsory purchase of much land. It opened in 1962 but, in a remarkable about turn, by British Rail, the Swanbourne yard was never built – no doubt much to the relief of the local inhabitants.

Next came Winslow which, before Verney Junction station opened in 1868, was an important place for changing between the Banbury and Oxford routes. For this reason sizeable waiting rooms were built on the up side. Winslow station had a spacious approach road with a circular drive around a green with a delightful horse chestnut tree. When visited in May 1990 the up platform and building were still there but in a derelict state. A few tiles were left on the building's roof and, where once passengers waited by welcoming coal fires, now grew pussy willow, cherry and ivy. A single track remained, used by freight trains. A notice advertised Milton Keynes shopping specials which ran in November 1990 – a welcome sight on a line closed to passengers in January 1968.

Verney Junction with its three platforms served not only the Buckingham Railway but, from 1868, it became a terminus for trains from Aylesbury via Quainton Road. Situated in an utterly remote location, its only neighbours were a few houses and 'The

33

Verney Arms'. Yet Verney Junction station is no more. An over-grown platform edge faces the single freight line although 'Station House' with its date of 1870 is today a private residence and the ticket office is a garage.

Towards Oxford, the next intermediate station was Claydon. When visited only the platform remained and the level crossing was operated by lights. At the entrance to the former station approach a pillar box read 'Claydon Station'. Not far away was Claydon House, a 16th century manor house owned by the Verney family, although much altered over the years. The house is today National Trust property where visitors can enjoy the magnificent staterooms with their carvings and visit a museum with momentoes of the Verney family and Florence Nightingale who was a sister of Parthenope, Lady Verney, and who often stayed there.

The last major station was at Bicester in Oxfordshire. This became Bicester, London Road in 1954 and when it closed in 1968 it seemed this was the end. Yet today, known as Bicester Town, passenger trains call once again with three coach DMUs

Bicester (London Road) station in the 1960s. Bicester has two stations, the other known today as Bicester North on the former GWR route from Princes Risborough to Banbury. (Lens of Sutton)

When Bicester London Road closed in 1968 it seemed to be the end but from 1989 services to Oxford have recommenced. The station is today known as Bicester Town and three coach DMUs provide seven trains daily. (Author)

34

providing seven trains daily to Oxford, a service jointly funded by local councils and Network South East. A plaque on the single platform read, 'Councillor Bryan Duggan, Chairman of Oxfordshire County Council, unveiled this plaque on 13th May 1989'. There was also hope further along the line. Passenger Transport Committees are trying to reinstate passenger services to Bletchley – hoping to eventually reach Peterborough.

Travelling the route from Verney Junction to Banbury, all that could be found at the former Padbury station was an old sleeper in the grass and a bulldog which took exception to the author! At Buckingham the station site had become a wooded walk with the platform edge just visible in the grass. No trace could be found of either Radclive or Water Stratford halts (opened in August 1956) whereas at Westbury Crossing (renamed Fulwell & Westbury in October 1880) the platform was still much in evidence. This was an attractive location with the bare brick platform flanking a farm track. In one direction the trackbed passed a line of poplars and towards Banbury was the crossing keeper's house. A local tractor-

Oxford (Rewly Road) station which closed to passenger services in 1951 when the Bicester trains were diverted to and from the GWR station. When photographed here in the 1960s it had become a freight depot. (Lens of Sutton)

Banbury (Merton Street) station, opened on 1st May 1850 as the northern terminus of the Buckingham Railway. The locomotive, seen here around 1950, was an ex-LMS 2-6-4T designed by W A Stanier and introduced in 1935. (Lens of Sutton)

35

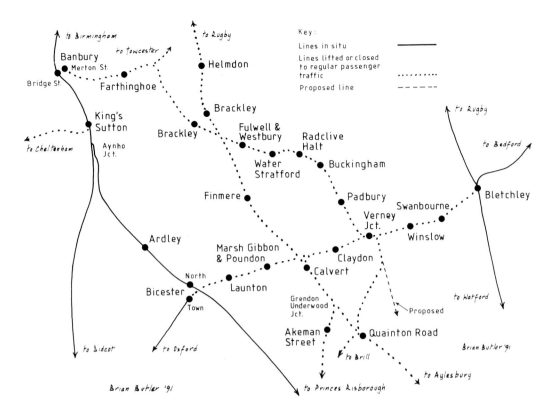

driver reminisced over the joys of once travelling such a pictures-que line.

Passenger traffic over the two routes was never very heavy although goods traffic proved useful. When the motor bus pro-vided competition and then the private motor car in the 1920s and 1930s, passenger levels dropped. In 1952 BR reduced the service but traffic increased once again when lightweight single-unit diesel cars were introduced in 1956 between Banbury and Buckingham. Despite this, BR claimed that the section remained uneconomic and closure came on 2nd January 1961. The line between Buck-ingham and Verney Junction survived a further three years to finally close on 7th September 1964. The line from Oxford to Bletchley fared little better closing on 1st January 1968. When the last train ran it was nearly empty and only a few exploding detonators marked the closure. It was a sad ending for a line that will perhaps one day return to life.

Chapter 5

NORTHWARDS TO RUGBY AND A BRANCH THROUGH WOTTON

(Quainton Road/Brackley/Woodford/Rugby and Ashendon Jct to Grendon Underwood Jct)

The Manchester, Sheffield & Lincolnshire Railway (MS&LR) began its existence as a provincial company providing a link across the Pennines and reaching Grimsby to the east. Its chairman, Sir Edward Watkin, was however an ambitious man for, by the end of the 1880s, he was also serving as chairman to the Metropolitan, South Eastern and East London Railways. One of his aims was to build a route to reach London from the MS&LR to run from Annesley, north of Nottingham, to Quainton Road, north of Aylesbury. At this point it would join existing tracks (later absorbed by the Metropolitan Railway) to reach the London terminus of Marylebone.

The section from Quainton Road to Rugby, almost 40 miles in length, received Parliamentary approval at a second attempt on 28th March 1893. The line was expensive to build requiring some 5,000 men, 150 horses, 50 locomotives and 1,700 wagons. South of Brackley a 252 yard viaduct was needed to cross the Great Ouse valley. The line was clearly a gamble particularly since the MS&LR was forever short of finance. Indeed the reputation of the company gave rise to rumours that the initials MS&L stood for 'money sunk and lost' and in 1891 the MS&LR changed its name to the Great Central Railway (GCR).

Calvert on the GCR Aylesbury-Rugby line in the early 1960s. The station closed to passengers on 4th March 1963 but track still remains today serving a waste terminal. (Lens of Sutton)

The line opened to passenger traffic on 15th March 1899 with goods traffic beginning a month later on 11th April. In their book *Forgotten Railways, Chilterns & Cotswolds*, R Davies and M D Grant wrote of a ceremonial opening which took place on March 9th when many assembled on platforms to watch special trains from Manchester, Sheffield and Nottingham pass through. At Woodford the local schoolchildren were given a half-day's holiday in honour of the event and were taken to the station by their schoolmaster where they were given flags by the station-master. The trains passed through to a salvo of fog signals and to the cheers of the children. In fact two of the trains ran late because of overheating in the axle boxes of the new coaches and the luncheon at Marylebone had to be taken before the official opening ceremony instead of after it.

The new line disappointed its promoters. It ran through thinly-populated agricultural areas and, in consequence, trains were usually lightly loaded and few in number, with initially twelve passenger trains daily between London and Nottingham and eleven in the up direction. Four trains ran each way on Sundays. A typical express from London Marylebone was the 6.20 pm which reached Nottingham (126½ miles) in 1 hour 45 minutes, slipping a coach at Leicester. The line benefited when a branch from Woodford to Banbury was opened on 13th August 1900 to link with the GWR which had provided financial assistance in return for the GCR's abandonment of support for a proposed London & South Wales Railway which, if constructed, would have been to the GWR's disadvantage.

The GCR further benefited in 1900 with the appointment of J G Robinson as locomotive designer and the company came to possess some fine engines. His first was a class 9J 0-6-0 used for goods traffic and this was followed by class 11B 4-4-0 for express

Station staff pose proudly as a passenger train approaches Brackley Central station c1910. The locomotive was probably a 4-4-0 Pollitt. Brackley was a relatively small town but it was served by seven trains a day to London including one express. (Lens of Sutton)

passenger trains. Perhaps his best known locomotive was the class 11E 4-4-0 of 1913 known as the *Directors*. Two years later Sam Fay was appointed as general manager and he soon earned much respect. By 1920 there were up to nine expresses daily each way between London and Nottingham with at least four including restaurant cars. The GCR earned a good reputation for punctuality and speed, beating the LNWR run to Rugby by two minutes and the Midland Railway to Leicester by four minutes.

On 20th November 1905 a six-mile double-track line opened to goods traffic between Grendon Underwood junction and Ashendon junction, connecting the GCR line with the Great Western & Great Central joint line north of Princes Risborough. Over four months later on 2nd April 1906, the line opened to passengers. The route via High Wycombe gave the GCR easier access to the capital, with a straighter track and with lesser gradients than on the Metropolitan line via Amersham. In addition staff on the Metropolitan route had frequently obstructed GCR workings. However, little traffic resulted on the diversion and the line finally closed to passengers in December 1953.

When 'grouping' came in 1923 the GCR became part of the

A general view of Brackley's GCR station c1910. Brackley's first station was opened by the LNWR in 1850 but the GCR line took away much of the LNWR traffic with its faster route to London when its passenger services commenced in 1899. (Lens of Sutton)

Brackley's Central station building in May 1991, some 25 years after closure. The property is today an ATS motoring centre and to the south the once well known viaduct has been demolished. (Author)

London & North Eastern Railway (LNER) which provided A3 'Pacifics' to haul its express trains. As steam trains came to an end, many kinds of locomotives could be seen including *Royal Scot* 4-4-0s, *Stanier Black* 5s plus BR Standard Class 4 2-6-0s and Class 5 4-6-0s. Occasionally a *Britannia Pacific* could be seen. In 1965 diesel multiple train units were introduced between Nottingham and London with extra trains between Woodford and Nottingham. On Sundays only one train ran in each direction. Freight traffic was considerable with much of it coal from the East Midlands. At Woodford there were as many as thirty three sidings for north-bound traffic and ten for the south.

By the early 1960s doubts were being raised over the future of the line. BR claimed a 'deteriorating financial position' while an ASLEF meeting in August 1962 passed a strongly worded protest to the Minister of Transport asking that complete closure should be refuted. Allegations were made that the government was deliberately running down the line so that it could be closed. When the Beeching Report was announced, the end was in sight. Last minute attempts were made to gain a reprieve but there was no hope and the Minister, Mrs Barbara Castle, made her decision. The last train ran on Saturday, 3rd September 1966.

Today sections of the former GCR line can be walked but at times the going can be tough. Brackley station building serves as an ATS motoring centre but to the south the once-great viaduct has been demolished. At Finmere a road underbridge has survived and tracks still pass through Calvert, where nearby pits are filled with rubbish from much of the south of England. The island platform is still there but instead of the buildings it is grass covered with a fair display of cowslips. The porters' room which was in the centre arch of the road bridge has gone but the white paint on the ceiling

Rugby's LNWR northern platform during the First World War. Rugby's Central line station, although some distance from the town centre, was nearby but this finally closed to passengers on 5th May 1969. (Lens of Sutton)

Wotton station building, formerly on the GCR link between Ashendon junction and Grendon Underwood junction, has been converted to an attractive private residence called 'The Old Station'. Before renovation the building housed chickens! (Author)

can still be seen. The bridge itself, when visited, was in danger of cracking causing concern over an asbestos mains water pipe which crossed at this point. Quainton Road has become the headquarters of the Buckinghamshire Railway Centre where many fine locomotives can be seen (see chapter 6).

From Calvert a spur still exists, put in during the Second World War enabling freight to join the Oxford–Bletchley line. On the link between Calvert and the GW & GC jt line towards Haddenham, track has survived only as far as a fertilizer plant at Woodham close to where Akeman Street station once stood. This railhead occasionally becomes a diesel loco-spotters paradise and there are plans to construct a loop in the plant area to allow run-round. Akeman Street station has gone and only the station master's house remains. After closure, Wotton station (GCR) building to the south became derelict and in the 1970s it housed chickens. Today it has been tastefully restored to a fine private dwelling called appropriately 'The Old Station'. The track crossed the road at this point and in the station there were four lines of track including sidings to a coal merchant's. The adjacent station master's house is today 'The Station House'. This was also the area where the track crossed the Wotton Tramway (see chapter 8) with that station's stables only a short distance away.

The GCR line to Rugby began as Sir Edward Watkin's dream of a rapid link between the Midland and the Channel ports. Some time ago a Labour transport spokesman recommended that the route should be re-opened to provide a fast through route to the Midlands when the Channel Tunnel is built. If this were to come about, then Sir Edward Watkin's dream will have come true.

Chapter 6

STEAM AT QUAINTON ROAD

(The Buckinghamshire Railway Centre)

Quainton Road station was at one time an outpost of London Transport, when Metropolitan trains ran from Baker Street through Quainton Road to Verney Junction. When the station first opened in 1868 it was part of the Aylesbury & Buckingham Railway (chapter 7) which was taken over by the Metropolitan in 1891. The station's existing buildings were constructed in 1896. Yet Quainton Road had another important role. The line was also part of the Great Central Railway (GCR) which from 1899 carried main-line trains between the Midlands and London Marylebone (chapter 5). This line was part of Sir Edward Watkin's dream that one day trains from the Midlands and North would use the route to cross London eventually reaching Paris through a Channel tunnel – still to be built! Sir Edward was not only a director of the GCR, but also of the Metropolitan and of the London, Chatham & Dover Railway Company (LCDR).

Quainton Road in the early 1960s, in its humbler BR days. In September 1966 the entire stretch from Aylesbury to Nottingham closed leaving only the former 'up' line to Calvert junction. (Lens of Sutton)

A third line also played a role at Quainton Road. The wooden building standing on platforms 2 and 3 was once a shelter for passengers waiting for trams on the Wotton Tramway – a private system opened in 1871 for the Duke of Buckingham's estate and by 1872 trams had reached Brill (chapter 8). Initially there was no direct connection between the tramway and Quainton Road although a turntable did connect with a siding. A bay platform

(which is today Quainton Road's platform 3) was provided in 1896 for the branch. Like the line to Verney Junction, the tramway also became part of the Metropolitan.

Platform three at Quainton Road where at one time trains left for the Brill branch. The branch first opened as the Wotton Tramway in 1871, a private line built for the Duke of Buckingham's Estate. (Author)

The Buckinghamshire Railway Centre was started by the London Railway Preservation Society in 1962. Items of historical railway equipment were collected and temporarily stored at government depots at Luton and Bishop's Stortford but space soon became a problem and a new and permanent home was needed. Many sites were visited and eventually Quainton Road station with its two large goods yards was selected. Quainton Road station closed to passengers on 4th March 1963 and just over three years later, on 3rd September 1966, the whole line from Aylesbury to Nottingham was closed with Quainton Road keeping only its former 'up' line as far as Calvert junction. In 1969, to protect members, Quainton Railway Society Ltd was formed and the London Railway Preservation Society was formally incorporated into the society on 24th April 1971. It is this society that was granted charitable status the following year. Quainton Road station yards are known today as the Buckingham Railway Centre.

When the society first moved to the site there was much to be done. No covered accommodation was available so a building was erected in the 'down' yard spanning three 150 ft long tracks to include workshops, a museum and a mess room. At the same time a building was acquired from London Transport, dismantled and transported from Wembley Park, and re-erected at the southern end of the yard. This became known as 'the Wembley Shed' and is used to house relics awaiting restoration and sometimes for special exhibitions. More buildings and exhibits followed, including a 60 ft turntable which the society hopes to install in the near future.

The society's present stock list is formidable. As well as many industrial locomotives, there are about a dozen main line locomotives with a number either undergoing overhaul or away on loan elsewhere. One of the locomotives at Quainton Road when visited by the author was *Metropolitan 1*, the only survivor of its class which was used on the Baker Street to Verney Junction service. The locomotive, an E class 0-4-4T, saw many years of duty on the MET line although when the MET electrification programme was completed such engines were less necessary. After removal of the condensing apparatus (fitted for working in underground tunnels) this class continued for a time on ballast and works trains with *Metropolitan 1* hauling its last steam-hauled train (as London Transport L44) in 1961. Two years later it was withdrawn but it had a moment of glory when it took part in the Metropolitan Centenary parade at Neasden in 1963.

Newly restored, *Metropolitan 1* starred during visits to the London Underground in July 1989 for Chesham branch centenary celebrations, and again in July 1990, when it hauled a special train to Stanmore on the Jubilee line. It travelled the inner rail Circle line via St James's Park in the small hours of the morning (much to the astonishment of night workers) en route to an open day at Upminster Depot.

In March 1973 a further important acquisition was made when GWR King Class 4-6-0 no 6024 *King Edward I* arrived at Quainton Road. During the late 1920s faster and heavier trains were being introduced on the country's major routes and to cope with these duties the GWR introduced its King class. Thirty were built to a design of C B Collett between 1927 and 1930. During its working life *King Edward I* covered over one and a half million miles hauling such prestige trains as the *Cornish Riviera Express* and the *Red Dragon*. The class was withdrawn in 1956 and, despite modifications, in 1962 BR condemned the locomotive for scrap at Barry. After eleven years of neglect it was rescued by the 6024 Preservation Society and a painstaking restoration began. Sixteen

Quainton Road was at one time an outpost of the Metropolitan Railway where trains passed through to Verney Junction and the preserved station today has kept this image. The single track serves BR freight. (Author)

44

years later, in 1989, efforts were rewarded when it could be seen 'running in' at Quainton Road. In May 1991 the locomotive was away on loan to the Birmingham Railway Museum and available for BR main-line running.

A visitor to Quainton Road will also find numerous coaches of interest. Beyond the display area on the 'up' side can be found a three coach set of London Transport CO/CP stock of 1938 vintage, used on the surface and sub-surface lines of the Underground until the early 1980s. The coach at the Aylesbury end, no 542433, is the remains of two trains partially destroyed in air raids in 1940, one at Plaistow Depot on 7th September and the other at Neasden Depot on 18th September. Since vehicles could not be easily replaced during the war, it was decided to join the two together and the rebuilt car entered service in September 1941. Withdrawn in February 1981, it came to Quainton in October and, halfway along the chassis, visitors can see where the two halves were joined.

In the main restoration shed can be found a four-wheeled vintage vehicle restored to a very fine standard. The woodwork and seating must surely be as good as new. This is LCDR 1st no 9, built c1880 at the Longhedge, Battersea, works of the LCDR. In the 1920s it was sold to Woolwich Arsenal for use on an internal railway system and when Quainton Road acquired it in 1962 it cost them a mere £7! Next to the LCDR coach is a relic of the Manchester, Sheffield & Lincolnshire Railway dating back to 1890. Also recently restored, this is a six-wheeled coach used on joint service with the LNWR. Later taken into GCR stock, it was transferred to the LNER in 1923 but withdrawn in the 1930s to become a camping coach. After twenty years subsequent use as a mess room at Victoria Dock, Hull, it might have been considered to be near its end but salvation came when it arrived at Quainton Road in 1971.

An unusual item of interest is the steam rail-car on the 'up' side

Quainton Road station closed to passengers on 4th March 1963 but has today become the Buckinghamshire Railway Centre with many exciting exhibits. Here it is possible to recapture the past and the days of steam. (Author)

Metropolitan Railway class E 0-4-4T no 1, the only survivor of a class of seven engines, heads LNWR 1st class dining car at the Buckinghamshire Railway Centre at Quainton Road. (T Davey)

built for the Egyptian State Railways in 1951 which had been stored at a depot south of Cairo for fifteen years before being purchased by the Sentinel Trust and transported to the UK in 1984. The boiler appeared to be in excellent condition and restoration of the three-car unit proceeds well. A short distance away can be found the Vale of Aylesbury Model Engineers miniature railway providing an enjoyable ride on a quarter of a mile of three gauge track. This is certainly not just for children but a fascination for 'grown-ups' as well where various model locomotives, faithful in every detail, leave 'Golden Springs Central' station at regular intervals.

There is much to commend a visit to Quainton Road. Set in splendid countryside and easily reached by car, it is well signposted off the A41 at Waddesdon. Enthusiasm in all departments is apparent and much credit is due to the many members who since 1969 have shared in making Quainton Road such a success. But there is still much to do and new members are always welcomed with training given for the many and varied duties members may perform. It has not been possible in this chapter to adequately cover the many exciting items to be discovered during a visit to the Buckinghamshire Railway Centre at Quainton Road so an early visit is strongly recommended.

Chapter 7

THE METROPOLITAN RAILWAY

(Baker Street/Rickmansworth/Aylesbury/Verney Junction and
Branches to Stanmore, Uxbridge, Watford and Chesham)

'Cheap day return tickets to the Chiltern country are issued from
all Underground stations on the Metropolitan and East London
lines. Rickmansworth 2/3 (just over 11p), Chorley Wood 2/6
(12½p) ... Stoke Mandeville 4/6 (22½p). Good Spot, the Chilterns. London Transport'. So read a poster attracting London folk
under the banner 'Away by Metropolitan' with promises that
included 'delightful country walks'. 'Looking for a house? Try
Rickmansworth' read another, offering a 'region of green hillsides
and woods where houses and sites are plentiful. See more of the
country by living on the Underground'. In the area which became
known as 'Metroland', in the 1930s quality houses could be
purchased from around £985, cheap by today's standards, to
include all legal fees with 90% mortgages arranged.

In the 1850s London's streets were frequently jammed with
slow-moving traffic and it was left to a City solicitor, Charles
Pearson, to find a solution. This came with the advent of a railway
to be built below the surface of the streets although raising capital
proved a major problem. Part of this came from the Great Western
Railway (GWR) which had more than a passing interest in the
project since it saw a means to get its trains from Paddington

LNER class N2 0-6-2T locomotives nos 4609 and 4742 at King's Cross c1930. The engines were fitted with condensing apparatus to reduce exhaust steam to permit working on underground Metropolitan lines to Moorgate. (Lens of Sutton)

Staff pose proudly on the up-platform at Rickmansworth MET station, c1910. In 1925 electrification reached Rickmansworth and the station became an electric and steam locomotive change-over point. (Lens of Sutton)

through to the City. In 1853 the Metropolitan Railway Company (MET) was formed. There was immediate concern from residents that tunnels would collapse or that passengers would be asphyxiated! Despite such fears a 3½ mile line was constructed between Bishop's Road (Paddington) and Farringdon Street and the world's first underground railway opened on 10th January 1863. The following year trains reached Hammersmith and Kensington, today known as Kensington (Olympia).

There were great celebrations and a banquet was held but troubles were soon experienced. With steam trains working the line the tunnels became heavily coated with soot and the persistent smoke upset staff and passengers alike. Staff were given permission to grow beards as a protection against the fumes! By the time City lines were completed, the MET had looked further afield and, anticipating lucrative goods and passenger traffic beyond Finchley Road, a line was built outwards from Baker Street. St John's Wood and Swiss Cottage were reached by 1868 and Willesden Green by 1879 – after Finchley Road tracks were mostly overground. The next objective was Harrow-on-the-Hill where a station building of modified Queen Anne style was constructed with booking offices and waiting rooms having the luxury of stained glass windows. When the station opened on 2nd August 1880, 36 trains ran daily to and from Baker Street with a generous Sunday service.

The directors continued to extend the MET with the Chilterns next in their sights. To achieve this, the Harrow & Rickmansworth Railway was incorporated in 1874 with trains reaching Rickmansworth on 1st September 1887. Meantime, in 1884, the Inner Circle, jointly owned by the Metropolitan and District Railways, was completed, plus a line to Aldgate East and St Mary's (Whi-

London Transport locomotive L44 (now Metropolitan 1 at Quainton Road) at Rickmansworth in 1950. In the background, one of the Metropolitan electric locomotives used to haul trains from Rickmansworth to Baker Street or beyond. (D K Jones)

techapel). There had been serious disagreements between the MET and the Metropolitan District Railway (known as the 'District') and it was because of this that completion had been delayed. On the first day MET trains ran on the (clockwise) outer rail and District trains on the (anti-clockwise) inner.

Looking outwards again, the next place of any importance was Chesham and MET trains reached the town on 8th July 1889. The section from Chalfont Road (renamed Chalfont & Latimer in November 1915) was always intended to be a single branch line. It became clear that the MET was looking towards Aylesbury as its prime objective but Chesham welcomed the trains and donated £2,000 towards the cost of a station to ensure it would reach the town centre and not the outskirts as originally planned. There had in fact been a proposal that the line would continue to Berkhamsted and, although 1½ miles of land was purchased beyond Chesham, the extension was never built. Chesham's train service was good with some reaching Baker Street in only 50 minutes – rivalling the trains of today. The station also provided many 'specials' with some worked through to Crystal Palace. A recollection of the branch can be found by a visit to the Bluebell Railway at Sheffield Park in Sussex where a 'Chesham set' of coaches is housed in the carriage shed at Horsted Keynes awaiting renovation.

As expected, Aylesbury was the next destination to be reached. Services commenced on 1st September 1892 but the town already had a railway, a link with Cheddington provided by the Aylesbury Railway (later LNWR) opened in 1839 (chapter 10). Yet another had come in 1863 when a GWR broad-gauge line reached Aylesbury from Princes Risborough. Both these earlier lines reached London by indirect routes and the MET had little to fear from competition. To the north of Aylesbury a further line had been opened in 1868 by a company called the Aylesbury & Buckingham Railway (A&BR) with its single line worked by the GWR. The railway started from a junction on the Oxford to Bletchley line (later to be known as Verney Junction) to reach Aylesbury via Quainton Road. Traffic was initially almost non-existent since Verney Junction was isolated in a very rural locality without even a small village. The MET, however, saw an opportunity and took over the line in 1891, doubling the track by 1897.

Another remote MET outpost was yet to come. The Brill branch, previously known as the Wotton Tramway, had opened in 1871 with the possibility envisaged in an Act of 1883 that it might eventually reach Oxford (see chapter 8). Although this never came about, the MET foresaw a lucrative branch should it be completed. On 1st December 1899 the Oxford and Aylesbury Tramroad (O&AT), as it optimistically became known, made over the working of the line to the MET, the O&AT remaining the proprietors. The branch had no signalling and worked on the 'one engine in steam' principle. The line was single throughout and there were numerous crossings, some of which had no keepers, leaving the fireman or guard to open and close the gates. The MET worked the line with redundant A class locomotives hauling either a mixed train or a single coach.

An important event in the history of the MET came in 1899 when the Great Central Railway (GCR) opened a line between Rugby and Quainton Road as part of Sir Edward Watkin's bid to link the North and Midlands with London – and beyond to Paris (see chapter 5). Sir Edward no doubt considered that a union with the MET would provide the ready-made link he required but the MET was not happy about the finances of the GCR (formerly the Manchester, Sheffield & Lincolnshire Railway) and a joint company never materialised. Instead the GCR was granted running powers over MET tracks between Quainton Road and Harrow-on-the-Hill but further south the MET refused to allow GCR trains to serve any station. There was continual bad feeling between the two companies and this was partly the reason why the new GCR line from Grendon Underwood junction (south of Calvert) to London via High Wycombe came about in 1906. To the south of Harrow therefore, it was agreed the GCR would use further tracks especially built by the MET and leased to the GCR for its exclusive use to and from Marylebone. The running of the line from Quainton Road to Harrow was undertaken by the Metropolitan & Great Central Joint Committee (M&GC jt) from April 1906.

Meanwhile, on 4th July 1904, the MET opened a branch from Harrow-on-the-Hill to Uxbridge. The Harrow & Uxbridge Railway Company had already been formed in 1897 and it was the opening of a line to South Harrow by the rival District Railway in 1903 that accelerated the MET's action. An intermediate station was opened at Ruislip and at various times numerous halts were opened to encourage traffic in the sparse countryside. In 1910, partly to overcome the bitter rivalry between the MET and the District, a spur was built from a halt at Rayners Lane (opened in May 1906) to connect with the District line at South Harrow although initially it was used solely to carry coal to a gasworks. The line subsequently carried District (later Piccadilly line) trains to Uxbridge with running powers over the MET tracks. An unusual aspect of the spur was that, although owned by the MET, it never carried any MET trains.

There was a spectacular accident on 23rd December 1904 when a north-bound parcels train from Marylebone, hauled by a Robinson 4-4-0 no 1040, left the track at Aylesbury. It was a foggy night and the train entered the station travelling at such a speed that it derailed and mounted the platform. Immediately an up Manchester train ploughed into the wreckage but fortunately at a slow speed and little extra damage was done. The parcels train driver died later in hospital. One of the vans had been loaded with Christmas puddings and it was reported that some of the people of Aylesbury lent more than a willing hand in helping to clear the line.

Electrification came to the MET on 1st January 1905 when the first multiple-unit service began between Baker Street and Harrow, also serving the Harrow to Uxbridge branch. Parliament had in fact approved electrification of the whole MET line in 1882 and various experiments were carried out. It was partly the cost of such a conversion that held the MET back and it was only when a competitor, the Central London Railway, opened electric lines in 1900 that the MET decided to act. Even then there was a strong disagreement with the 'District'. The MET decided on a 3-phase AC system, not previously attempted in this country, whereas the District was pressing for a tried and tested DC system. Violent arguments led the District to offer a take-over of the MET, offering a 3% interest to guarantee a DC system. The MET turned down the offer and eventually the dispute went to arbitration, with the Board of Trade

Ex LNER (GCR) class A5 4-6-2T (as BR 69807) awaiting in a bay at Rickmansworth to take over a MET train to Aylesbury. (D K Jones)

A GCR 4-6-2T class 9N (LNER class A5) locomotive at Chesham station. The engine was designed by J G Robinson and was built in 1911. MET trains first reached Chesham in 1889. (Lens of Sutton)

deciding on DC. A voltage of 600 was adopted plus a four rail system with the positive rail outside and the negative rail (insulated from earth) in the centre. The latter was a requirement of the Board of Trade used partly in respect of voltage drop and also to allow track circuiting for a proposed signalling system.

The first electric cars were built by the Metropolitan Amalgamated Carriage & Wagon Company with these open cars comparing well with the earlier narrow compartments used on the MET – often described as 'knee-knockers'. Entry was via a gated platform but especially during rush-hours, this was found unsatisfactory and sliding doors replaced the gates. The coaches, all 52 ft 6 in long, accommodated 49 passengers with seats arranged transversely and longitudinally. Over the next few years, further stock with only slight differences was ordered from various suppliers and in addition certain steam bogie stock was converted. The first ten electric locomotives, 'camel-back' types each carried on two motor bogies, were built between 1904 and 1906. A further ten of the same type, capable of handling heavier main line trains, were purchased in 1907 from British Thomson Houston (BTH). To allow working over non-electrified lines, these were changed for steam locomotives at Wembley Park or Harrow.

The MET could claim a number of innovations during its early existence. In the book, *The Metropolitan Railway*, C Baker wrote that in 1906 the company pioneered automatic coin-operated ticket machines at Farringdon Street. A special saloon was built for Lord Rothschild from two small compartment coaches containing cooking and toilet facilities plus a compartment for attendants. It could be used for special parties and was at the disposal of the directors. Another achievement was a contract with the Pullman Car Company to run buffet cars on business trains and late-night theatre runs. This service began in June 1910 with the two Pullman cars *Galatea* and *Mayflower*. The supplement to the first-class fare from London was 6d (2½p) to Rickmansworth and 1/– (5p) beyond. The cars reached the extremes of the MET travelling

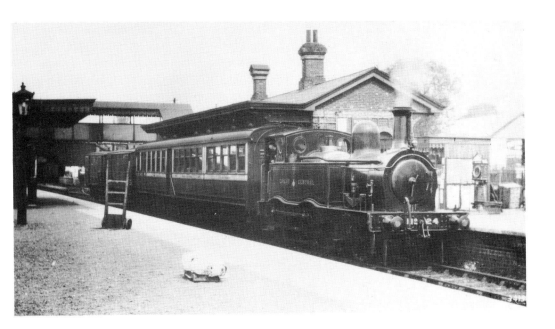

Aylesbury station c1910 where a GCR train awaits departure. The locomotive, ex-Manchester, Sheffield & Lincoln Railway 2-4-0T no 24, hauls a mixed passenger and freight load. (Lens of Sutton)

from the City and Baker Street to Chesham and to far-flung Verney Junction, nearly 60 miles from Aldgate.

As services improved, demand on the electric locomotives grew. Batches were withdrawn from 1922 and sent to Vickers Ltd at Barrow-in-Furness for reconstruction returning with very little of the original left. Immediate needs were met when new locomotives were delivered, having four 300 hp motors, two in each bogie, giving 1,200 hp in all. They were painted chocolate and lined in black and yellow. The locomotives could attain a maximum speed of 65 mph and were capable of fast acceleration from rest. They initially carried the word 'Metropolitan' between two coats of arms but later the word was replaced by a bronze plate bearing the name of a well known character associated with the MET. There were eventually twenty locomotives and only no 15 was different, being called 'Wembley 1924' to commemorate the exhibition, where it was shown with one side removed to display the internal equipment. On 5th January 1925 electrification reached Rickmansworth, with the station becoming an electric and steam locomotive change-over point.

For many years the MET had been aware that Watford, although already served by the LNWR (chapter 1), had sufficient potential to justify another rail service to London. Parliamentary approval was obtained in 1922 although construction proved difficult with some ten bridges required including two across the Grand Union canal and the river Colne. The cost of the branch was put at £300,000 and the line opened on 2nd November 1925 with electric trains worked by the MET and steam-hauled trains by the LNER (formerly GCR). Almost immediately there were around 140 trains daily but the futility of running steam trains over electric tracks was soon appreciated. The LNER withdrew its services after the General Strike of May 1926. Much publicity was given to the Watford branch – 'The New Route to Watford' read a MET advertisement. 'The new Metro, double-track extension line to Croxley Green and Watford, now open for traffic, offers many advantages to the travelling public. It makes Watford – Hertfordshire's largest and most important town – easier of access; opens up an unique residential district offering unlimited scope for building operations and, at the same time, materially improves London's transport facilities'.

A link was constructed between the intermediate station of Croxley Green and Rickmansworth so that Watford trains could work northwards without reversing and also allow a shuttle service of electric trains between Rickmansworth and Watford. There was concern that the MET's Watford terminus was in a quiet part of the town so four 28-seater Albion buses were purchased to meet trains and take passengers to the town centre. These were later sold to the subsidiary of a local bus company which subsequently amalgamated its interests with the Watford omnibus company of Frederick Lewis. A new company, the Lewis Omnibus Co Ltd, was formed which continued to operate until 1933.

A GCR 4-4-2 class 8B (LNER C4) no 260 passes through Waddesdon Manor in the 1930s. This class was built at Gorton in 1906, designed by J G Robinson, and they were nicknamed 'Jersey Lillies'. (Lens of Sutton)

In October 1927 the MET made a further attempt to reach the centre of Watford by purchasing a property at 44, Watford High Street, formerly the Empress Tea Rooms for £14,200. It was thought an extension would bring considerable extra revenue being so close to the shops and the market. A costly tunnel of approximately 1,100 yards would have been necessary and the project was abandoned. The building, formerly a Grange furniture store, is now a branch of Next Ltd. For a time the MET had been optimistic about the proposal and the building carried posters advertising a rail service to the West End and the City.

Waddesdon Manor station c1910. The station was not far from the National Trust property of that name which was built between 1874 and 1889 by Baron Ferdinand de Rothschild. The station closed in July 1936. (Lens of Sutton)

Throughout much of its life the Metropolitan Railway saw great opportunities in promoting growth in the area it served. Its first development, for rent, was the Cecil Park Estate at Pinner in the late 1880s but it was the opening of the Uxbridge line on 4th July 1904 that really launched the building boom. On that occasion an Uxbridge newspaper commented, 'Uxbridge is expected to grow into a first-class residential neighbourhood and a health resort'. From 1915 a publication called *Metroland*, issued annually, could be purchased along the line and in 1919, to further the building of houses, a subsidiary company, the Metropolitan Railway Country Estates Ltd, was formed. Houses were available from £500 freehold and MET estates included Moor Lane Estate, Rickmansworth; Cedars Estate, Rickmansworth; Chenies Estate, Chorley Wood; Chenies Estate, Little Chalfont; Beechwood Estate, Chalfont; and Weller Estate, Amersham. By the end of 1939 the MET Estates company had built more than 4,600 houses.

Late in the life of the MET there were plans to build a further branch to Stanmore and on to Elstree linking with the former Midland line from St Pancras. Only the 4½ mile stretch to Stanmore was completed leaving the main line half a mile north of Wembley Park station. At the opening ceremony on 10th December 1932, the train was a new multiple-unit set, plus a Pullman car and private saloon with the passengers including company officials and other dignitaries. Intermediate stations were built at Kingsbury and Canons Park, with Queensbury opening in December 1934. A frequent service of 144 trains was provided daily to attract passengers and many travelled the 6½ miles between Wembley Park and Baker Street nonstop. The branch was the first outside America to introduce centralised traffic control. Colour-light signals were installed, controlled from Wembley Park signal box where an illuminated diagram showed the position of the train. When in November 1939 a connection with the Bakerloo line was completed, Stanmore's MET trains were withdrawn and replaced by 'tube' trains to and from the Elephant & Castle. In May 1979

Verney Junction, the furthest outpost of the Metropolitan Railway, photographed in the 1960s. Despite its very rural location, this was an important junction where many lines met. (Lens of Sutton)

the Jubilee line opened between Charing Cross and Baker Street, and Wembley Park to Stanmore became a part.

On 1st July 1933 the MET passed into the ownership of the London Passenger Transport Board (LPTB). Locomotives including the handsome K class engines were repainted with the London Transport lettering and they continued their freight and passenger workings up to Verney Junction. In 1936 the LPTB launched a series of press advertisements to encourage trips to the Chilterns using the slogan 'Away by Metropolitan'. A typical advert read, 'Is there anywhere a view more glorious, more stirring, than from the top of Bacombe Hill and Coombe Hill on a clear Spring day? Is there?' Books on *Country Walks* were also produced to encourage trippers.

During the years up to the Second World War the MET as it was known slowly began to disintegrate. The Brill branch closed on 30th November 1935 and the line from Quainton Road to Verney Junction was reduced to single track and kept only for goods traffic. Building expansion had to slow down with the Green Belt protecting many open spaces and when the war came the 'Metro-dream' was at an end. There were many incidents during the air-raids mostly in the City section. Moorgate station was practically destroyed and bombs hit the tunnels, putting the line between Euston Square and King's Cross out of action for many weeks. There was also heavy damage at Baker Street and Kilburn. First-class facilities were withdrawn and the Pullman cars *Galatea* and *Mayflower* became things of the past.

After the war, on 1st January 1948, nationalisation meant that railways previously administered by the LPTB became part of the British Transport Commission (BTC). On 1st January 1963 a further change took place when the BTC was dissolved, its place taken by the new British Railways Board, with the London Underground under independent control (the London Transport Board). On 12th September 1960 electric trains reached Amersham and Chesham and on 9th September 1961, the last day of steam working on the London Transport, MET services were withdrawn north of Amersham. By June 1962 four-tracking had been completed as far north as Watford South junction. On 3rd September 1966 the last train ran on the former GCR line from Aylesbury to Rugby and the last vestige of Sir Edward Watkin's dream of a line to the south coast had gone. Aylesbury became an outpost of the former MET line served only by local diesel services from Marylebone via Rickmansworth or via High Wycombe.

July 1989 was the centenary month of the opening of the MET line between Rickmansworth and Chesham and E class 0-4-4T *Metropolitan 1* hauled a number of special trains between Watford and Chesham carrying a headboard reading 'Chesham 100 Years 1889–1989'. Beyond Aylesbury there are still many reminders of the past. The platform edges and a single track have survived at Waddesdon Manor (closed in July 1936) but at Quainton Road the many fine exhibits at the Buckinghamshire Railway Centre include *Metropolitan 1* (chapter 6). Grandborough Road's platform edges can still be determined and at Winslow Road the site has become 'Station Kennels'.

At Verney Junction there is little to see except surviving platform edges and the single freight line that runs from Bicester to Bletchley. Station House is still there carrying the date 1870 and the station ticket office has become a private garage. When visiting the area it seemed hard to believe that this was once a junction serving four different directions. Hard also to believe that the Pullman cars *Galatea* and *Mayflower* called at the station and that it was also once possible to book an excursion to places like Ramsgate.

The late Poet Laureate, Sir John Betjeman, loved the Metropolitan and wrote:

> Child of the First War, Forgotten by the Second,
> We called you Metro-land. We laid our schemes
> Lured by the lush brochure, down byways beckoned,
> To build at last the cottage of our dreams
> A City clerk turned countryman again.
> And linked to the Metropolis by train.

Chapter 8

A TRAMWAY BUILT FOR A DUKE

(Quainton Road to Brill)

The well-known National Trust property of Waddesdon Manor was built between 1874 and 1889 by Baron Ferdinand de Rothschild and designed in the French Renaissance style. The cone-shaped hilltop had previously been barren and the transformation was a considerable task. Bath stone and other building materials were brought by the Wotton Tramway from the railway at Quainton to Westcott from where the supplies were steam-winched across the field on tracks. From there a cable engine hauled the trucks up the hill to the summit where the cutting made for the incline track can still be seen.

The Wotton Tramway originated in the early 1870s to serve an estate of the Duke of Buckingham. Following completion of the A&BR's line from Aylesbury to Quainton Road in September 1868, work to build the tramway began. No Act of Parliament was needed since the majority of the track was laid on the Duke's land. The initial line was just under four miles long with goods traffic reaching Wotton on 1st April 1871. The track was standard gauge and, because it was primarily intended as a horse tramway, longitudinal sleepers were used. These came from Norwegian timber and were considered very tough. They were delivered to Quainton Road at a cost of 1/10d (approx 9p) per foot.

By November of that year the line was extended to a brickworks near Brill and a horse-worked 1½ mile spur, known as the

Ex-Metropolitan Railway class A 4-4-0T no 23 (built Beyer Peacock Ltd) leaves Quainton Road in the early 1930s on the Brill branch. This locomotive is preserved at the London Transport Museum at Covent Garden. (Lens of Sutton)

58

This wooden building, seen today at Quainton Road, was the shelter for passengers waiting for trains on the Brill Tramway, a private line built in 1871 for the Duke of Buckingham's estate. (Author)

Kingswood branch, was built to a coal wharf at Moate Farm on Kingswood Lane. There was criticism over the location of the wharf which was sited on low ground liable to flooding. It is said that the precise spot was chosen during an argument between the Duke and a surveyor. According to a local story, the Duke threw his hat and where it fell the wharf was built!

In January 1872 the company gave way to the folk of Brill who clamoured for a passenger service. For this, a 6 hp four-wheeled steam engine was purchased from Aveling & Porter of Rochester in Kent at a cost of £400 and a Great Western composite coach was borrowed. The engine had a running speed of up to 8 mph and there were soon complaints from drivers about exposure to the weather. Eventually cabs and running boards were added and spark arrester funnel caps were fitted. Water for the engine came from assorted lineside ponds and streams.

During the summer of 1872 the final section to Brill was completed giving a total route length of 6¼ miles and a second engine was acquired, similar to the first. It was now possible to run three mixed trains daily with another when required. Despite the sparse population, (at the time Wotton had only 220 inhabitants) the number of passengers carried was encouraging. From just over 100 in the first month, the figure rose to 224 during April 1872. Single fares from Quainton Road were 3d (just over 1p) to Westcott (earlier spelled Wescott), 6d (2½p) to Wotton and 1/– (5p) to Brill. Tickets were issued by the guard during the journey. There was no direct connection between the tramway and the Aylesbury & Buckingham Railway at Quainton Road although a turntable did connect with a siding. There was another turntable at Brill, installed after it was found that the engines ran better funnel first.

Times were hard for the staff. Rules laid down that each servant must 'devote himself exclusively to the service, attend regularly during the appointed hours and to refrain from using improper language, cursing or swearing ...' Smoking during duty was strictly prohibited and intoxication would render any employee liable to instant dismissal. If a driver did not have his engine ready for duty when required he could be fined one shilling (5p) and if the delay was partly the fault of his assistant he would pay a portion. The driver communicated with the guard by using his engine whistle. One short blast instructed the guard to apply the brakes, two meant release the brakes and a prolonged whistle was to draw the attention of roadmen on the line or at a station. Three prolonged blasts meant trouble, perhaps a fire on the train, a derailment or possibly a fire on adjacent land amongst crops.

In 1876/7 the company spent £1,240 with Bagnells of Stafford on saddle tank locomotives designed for use on light railways or tramways and named them *Buckingham* and *Wotton*. A few years later the line's only known fatal accident occurred. In his book *The Wotton Tramway (Brill Branch)*, Ken Jones wrote that on 8th March 1883 the lady's maid of the Duke of Buckingham's daughter was walking the line near Wotton with two other ladies' maids having just left the evening train from Quainton Road. As the train caught them up, the driver sounded his whistle and two moved aside. Unfortunately the third, Maria Nichols, lingered to watch the approaching train and was knocked down and killed instantly. The coroner's verdict was accidental death and the driver, James Challis, was cleared of all blame.

Also in 1883, a railway was planned which would have linked Quainton Road with Oxford. On 20th August Parliament agreed the incorporation of the Oxford, Aylesbury & Metropolitan Junction Railway Company. Its directors included the Duke of Buckingham and Sir Harry Verney, both important landowners. This was to be a branch from Sir Edward Watkin's new trunk route from the Midlands to the South of England and, at one stage, electric traction was considered.

Trains would have had running powers over the A&BR from Aylesbury and, from Quainton Road, tracks would have been constructed via Westcott, Brill and Swanton St John to a terminus in the High Street at St Clements, Oxford. Finance was scarce and five years later hardly any work had been done. A second Act was passed on 7th August 1888 which changed the name to the Oxford & Aylesbury Tramroad Company (O&AT), abandoned the railway project and agreed a tramroad extension. Despite this and two further Bills, Oxford was never reached.

The failure of this extension was partly due to the death of the Duke of Buckingham on 26th March 1889. The Duke's interests in the tramway were passed on to his nephew, Mr Gore Langton, Earl Temple. Little further changed over the next year or so – new locomotives were hired, derailments became frequent and the hot summer of 1893 saw a water shortage for the engines. To remedy this a 1,000 gallon water tank was built to supplement the supply.

When the O&AT took over the running in 1894, a new permanent way was constructed and stations were built. *Huddersfield*, a

Manning Wardle 0–6–0 saddle tank was bought and a similar locomotive was purchased later in the year, bearing the name *Earl Temple* in 3¾ inch letters on a brass plate. The tramway worked on the basis of 'one engine in steam' or two or more coupled together. Stations existed at Quainton Road, Waddesdon Road, Westcott, Wotton, Wood Siding (a simple waiting room only) and Brill, constructed with low platforms to suit the carriages. In 1896 Quainton Road station was resited when a bay platform was provided for Brill branch trains.

A class A 4-4-0T Beyer Peacock locomotive approaches Westcott station on the Brill branch. This engine was formerly used on the Metropolitan line but it became redundant with electrification. (Lens of Sutton)

In December 1899 the Metropolitan Railway acquired the lease of the tramway with an option to purchase, an option that was never taken up. The Metropolitan continued to work the line using

Today a private garage, this was once the original station building at Westcott which housed the toilets, the waiting room and the ticket office. The hatch and counter where tickets were purchased remain intact. (Author)

Wotton no 2 (purchased in February 1899) and *Brill no 1* (previously named *Earl Temple*). *Huddersfield* was found to be in poor condition and was sold for a low sum. The coach used was a 3rd class rigid-eight-wheeler previously hired by the O&AT from the Metropolitan Railway, since the original coach had become 'a little out of condition'. The Metropolitan coach had its gas fittings replaced by oil lamps and at Quainton Road the bay platform was modified to accommodate it.

Wotton no 2 failed in March 1903 and the new owners brought in a Sharp Stewart 2–4–0T class D engine. The track in the Brill yard was already in a poor condition but the new locomotive damaged it further and it needed replacing in August 1903 at a cost of £804. Derailments along the branch were so frequent that the Metropolitan introduced D class engines nos 71 and 72 from its Verney Junction–Aylesbury line and sold its two Manning Wardle engines, *Brill no 1* and *Wotton no 2*, to contractors.

With the Metropolitan tracks through Quainton Road forming part of the Great Central route to the North, it was logical that the two companies should combine. In August 1905 Parliament passed the Metropolitan & Great Central Railway Companies Act, thus establishing the Met & G C Joint Committee (M&GC jt) which took on the lease of the whole line from Harrow South junction to Verney Junction as from 2nd April 1906. A section in the Act included the Wotton Tramway, whereby the Joint Committee assumed the lease on the same date although final agreement was not reached until 11th June 1913.

Meantime under provisions in an Act of 1899, the Great Western & Great Central Joint Committee had received approval to build a railway from Princes Risborough to Grendon Underwood junction (north of Quainton Road on the GCR line) which would pass over the tramway at Wotton giving a second station. When this line opened to passengers in April 1906, the tramway lost many of its passengers with an alternative and fast route now available to London and later, using the GWR line via Banbury, to Birmingham.

At Wotton, not far from the GCR station building, the stables which housed horses that worked the sidings on the tramway can be found along a pathway. (Author)

The condition of the tramway track continued to cause concern and the M&GC jt were compelled to relay it. When completed the Board of Trade agreed that the speed limit could be raised to 25 mph although certain restrictions remained such as over level crossings where an 8 mph limit was maintained. With electrification coming to the Metropolitan's Underground lines, two redundant steam locomotives found their way to the tramway. These were class A 4–4–0T Beyer Peacock engines nos 23 and 41, and they took the place of the earlier D class engines.

The O&AT tried to sell the line but the M&GC jt was not interested since it was content to continue the leasing arrangement. In 1923 the O&AT had the line valued at £34,730. An approach was made to the GWR to purchase the tramway but after several months it decided against. Other moves proved equally futile and little further transpired until 1933 when the London Passenger Transport Board (LPTB) was formed, and the Metropolitan Railway and the District Railway came under one ownership. In 1935 the LPTB decided it was not prepared to continue suburban services to Aylesbury and beyond. The tramway (now known as the Brill branch) was to close.

The last train ran on 30th November 1935. *The Times* of 2nd December 1935 reported, 'For the last time an antiquated little tank engine drew an equally antiquated passenger coach along the line between Quainton Road and Brill. The train contained officials of the Metropolitan Railway Company including an assistant superintendent. It stopped at each of the five stations on the line. Documents, records and all valuables from each station were placed in the guards van and then the station lights were put out and the train steamed along to its destination at Quainton Road'. The railway, buildings and equipment were put up for sale with waiting rooms going for as little as £5 each. After over 60 years the tramway had reached a sad end.

Had the tramway reached Oxford then perhaps things might have been different. Today the track can be traced and numerous buildings have survived. At the Buckinghamshire Railway Centre

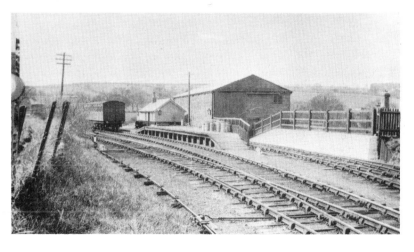

Brill station, the tramway's terminus c1910. The line opened initially for freight but commenced passenger services in January 1872 following pressure from Brill residents. (Lens of Sutton)

*One of the Aveling &
Porter engines, no 807,
that worked the Wotton
Tramway was rescued in
1951 by the Industrial
Locomotive Society and it
can be found today at the
London Transport
Museum at Covent
Garden. (Author)*

at Quainton Road the wooden waiting room on platforms 2 and 3 was once a shelter for passengers waiting for Brill trams and at Westcott the original station building has survived the years. Today a garage located at 'Station House', a private residence in the village, once housed the toilets, the waiting room and the booking office. Even the hatch and counter where tickets were purchased remains intact. In addition, the owner showed the author where pieces of track had been dug up in the adjacent garden. At Wotton (not far from the GCR station building – see chapter 5) only the stables survive where horses were housed which worked the sidings. Brill station building has gone but station houses carry the legends B&C (Buckingham and Chandos) 1871 and 1888. Nearby can be found Tramway Farm.

There is yet another tangible reminder of the tramway. When the Manning Wardle engines arrived in 1906, the two Aveling and Porters were left out in the open and abandoned. Eventually they were sold to a brickworks at Weedon in Northants where no 807 became a shunting engine until closure of the works in 1940. The second engine, no 846, was cannibalised to keep no 807 working. In 1951 the Industrial Locomotive Society rescued no 807 from the brickyard where it had been abandoned once again. After various homes, no 807 can today be found at the London Transport Museum at Covent Garden, where it stands resplendent, recalling its tramway days.

Chapter 9

A BRANCH TO NEWPORT PAGNELL AND A STEAM TRAMWAY

(Wolverton to Newport Pagnell and Wolverton to Stony Stratford)

Wolverton owes its existence largely to the fact that the London & Birmingham Railway Company chose it as a site for a new railway works. Sheds and workshops were opened in 1838 and the company also constructed houses, schools and a church for its employees. Later the railway (known as the London & North Western Railway – LNWR – from 16th July 1846) took its locomotive works to Crewe and the Wolverton works concentrated on carriage building requiring yet more employees. This, combined with the arrival in 1878 of the large printing and stationery works McCorquodale & Company, meant that adequate transport in the area had become an urgent necessity. McCorquodale's business was very transport orientated and rivalled the Bell Punch Company in the production of tickets for tramways as well as railways.

Wolverton to Newport Pagnell

Parliament agreed a four mile single track branch from Wolverton to Newport Pagnell on 16th June 1863. Just over two years later the first engine went down the line hauling 17 wagons each crammed with the navvies who had helped to build it but it was not until the following year that the railway opened for freight and cattle. Finally on 2nd September 1867 the great day came when passenger trains commenced services. The streets were decorated, church bells

Wolverton station which also served a line to Newport Pagnell until the branch closed in September 1964. Wolverton was at one time the site for a railway works for the London & Birmingham Railway but when this moved to Crewe the works concentrated on carriage building. (Lens of Sutton)

rang out and the Swan Hotel carried a huge illuminated star. At 1.15 pm a free trip to Wolverton was offered but so many turned up that hundreds were left behind on the platform. In the waiting room railway officials and their friends were served with champagne.

The LNWR worked the line and staff employed included an engine driver, a fireman and three permanent way men. The driver received 42/- (£2.10) per week and his fireman 24/6 (£1.22½) while permanent way men received between 17/- and 22/- (85p and £1.10). The two intermediate stations of Bradwell and Linford each employed one man who, in his spare time, delivered parcels within a mile of his station. Traffic was busy and the new service brought about the revival of the Newport Pagnell Steeplechase with special trains carrying spectators. Only one engine was allowed on the line at one time and the train became known as 'Nobby'.

There was a proposal that the branch should be extended to Olney on the Midland Railway line between Bedford and Northampton. Work began and a bridge over the Newport to Wolverton road was built. Further construction work was carried out along the route but the project was suddenly abandoned and all work stopped. In 1900 a spur was constructed close to Wolverton station to connect the branch with the up slow line. This formed an angle so that Royal Train coaches could be turned. A proposal to electrify the branch came from the LNWR in 1904 using the same system as that already used by three companies in the north of England. The LNWR considered such a move would bring about considerable saving but the idea did not materialise. Locally nobody really thought there would be an electrified Nobby.

Writing in *Country Railwaymen*, A E Grigg related a mishap from the late 1920s that could have had more serious consequences. There was no signal box at Newport Pagnell and the guard or station staff worked the main points and signals from a ground frame. The 5.20 pm train was about to leave Newport Pagnell

When the Newport Pagnell branch opened to passengers on 2nd September 1863, one man was employed at Bradwell. In his spare time he was expected to deliver parcels locally. (Lens of Sutton)

when the driver decided he would take on more coal. The engine was uncoupled, refilled in the shed and then taken back to the station for recoupling. Unfortunately the porter guard, having spent his time chatting to the passengers, forgot to change the points so when the train moved off, it returned to the coal shed and ran through the rear wall. The engine and carriages came to rest peacefully in a ditch especially placed to catch runaway trains.

No one was hurt, but a lady passenger carrying a basket full of eggs had a sticky mess to clear up. Being a single line, it was not possible to call upon another engine to assist without the train 'staff' or 'token'. Fortunately the fireman had a motorbike and so he set off for Wolverton with the train staff to arrange help. After considerable delay the train was reunited with the railway line and the porter guard was summoned to Derby to see his 'chief'. He naturally feared the worst and his colleagues wished him well. When he returned he was smiling, for instead of dismissal he had been offered promotion to passenger guard!

In the early 1940s the line was supplied with LNWR tank locomotives fitted with a vacuum regulator on the smoke box which enabled the driver to operate a push-pull 'motor-train'. By this means, the driver could sit in the leading coach driving compartment and, by various bell codes, tell the fireman when to open or close the regulator. The engine now pulled the train to Newport Pagnell and then pushed it back to Wolverton. At the same time it was agreed that 'Nobby' could become a mixed passenger and freight train and this became a common sight. The line was quite a family affair and everybody knew the members of staff. It was especially popular with the many schoolchildren who were regular travellers. Sometimes 'Nobby' was late because the steep gradient out of Newport Pagnell proved too much of a strain, particularly in frosty weather, and sometimes ash or sand had to be put on the track. Yet the train always made it in the end, even though late on arrival. This was the 'Happy-Go-Lucky Line'!

During the Second World War the shed-labourer, Joe Ashton,

The terminus at Newport Pagnell prior to its closure in 1964. During the previous century work began to extend the line to Olney but the project was soon abandoned. The branch track at the terminus was lifted during 1990 and today only the sign 'Station Road' shows where the site existed. (Lens of Sutton)

worked nights unloading coal. Some of this was used for coaling the engine so it was in steam ready for the first train next morning. On one occasion the driver decided he would give Joe a fright so, knowing Joe would move the locomotive around 2 am to where he could shovel coal into the bunker, he placed detonators in front of the engine. As expected the engine moved forward amidst successive loud bangs which echoed across the quiet countryside. At first Joe was not unduly concerned but he became very anxious when he saw, crossing the adjoining field, soldiers with rifles at the ready deployed in a pincer movement around the engine shed. The loud noise had alerted the Home Guard in their nearby headquarters.

The water supply for locomotives at Wolverton was at best no more than a trickle so drivers endeavoured to use a water column at the intermediate station of Bradwell. This water came from the town's supply and as Bradwell expanded, many of the houses at what became Top End, higher than the station, found that when the engine was taking water, they were losing their supply. On Mondays housewives often shook their fists at engine drivers when their weekly wash was interrupted. Eventually drivers were forbidden from taking water from Bradwell on a Monday. As more houses were built so the situation got worse and in the end the column wheel was padlocked.

When proposals to close the line were announced the people of Newport Pagnell were determined to fight. An enquiry was held on 7th June 1964 but, despite many forceful arguments, it was decreed that the line should go. On 5th September 1964, the ex-LMS 2–4–2T no 1222 waited with the 5.34 pm train from Newport Pagnell. Crowds watched as 'cleaners' gave 'Nobby' a final wash and brush up and accidentally emptied a bucket of water over Dr Beeching's double. Amidst cheers and long blasts on the whistle the train pulled away, and at Linford and Bradwell many mourned its passing. For a while freight trains continued and then they were discontinued as well.

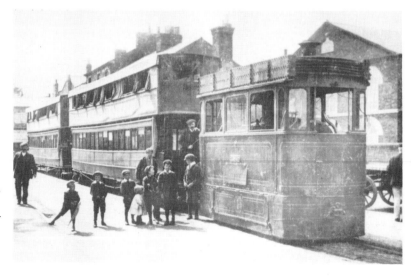

Wolverton & Stony Stratford's Green tram no 1 about to haul two 100-seater cars c1910. The sag in the cars through heavy loads is already beginning to show. (Lens of Sutton)

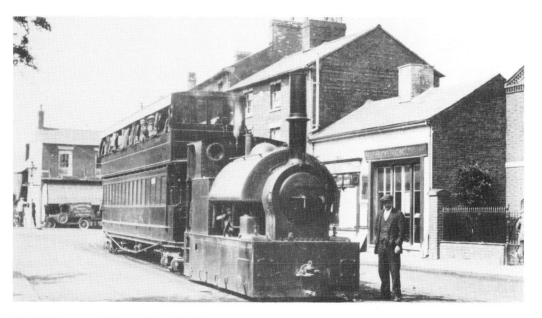

The Wolverton & Stony Stratford Tramway

Prior to the coming of the tramway, transport between Wolverton and Stony Stratford had been sparse with only a number of small horse buses making the journey. One, owned by Mr Rich, could carry only four passengers inside and two outside. Another 'bus', owned by Joseph Clare who was landlord at the Cock Inn in the High Street, could accommodate just two inside and two outside. Only a few doors away was the Bull Inn owned by Thomas Carter and there was much rivalry between the two landlords. Both became well known for their tall stories and it has been said that this is how the expression 'a cock and bull story' originated.

A first attempt to build a light railway came in November 1882 when the Wolverton & Stony Stratford Tramways Co Ltd was formed by local interests but it was not successful. In less than a year it was placed in voluntary liquidation, to be replaced on 6th September 1883 by the Wolverton & Stony Stratford & District Tramway Co Ltd. Meantime a Tramways Order had been sought by Frederick Charles Winby, a civil engineer and contractor. This was granted on 16th July 1883 authorising 2 miles 54 chains of single track, 4 ft gauge, between the towns. When incorporated, the new company acquired Winby's rights and interests in the Order. Winby undertook to build the line but, like the previous attempt, the endeavour fell through.

Eventually on 18th August 1886 serious progress was made. Charles Herbert Wilkinson of Wilkinson & Co, a local firm of contractors, had already shown interest in a number of schemes, including one to link Newport Pagnell and Olney and he agreed a contract to build the Wolverton line for £13,325. The name of the company was changed to the Wolverton, Stony Stratford & District Light Railways Co Ltd. The shares offered for sale were quickly taken up and work began.

Bagnall no 5 and a 100-seater car at the Foresters Arms awaiting departure to Wolverton. Note the bogies placed at the extreme end of the car so that the couplings remained central over the track when negotiating curves. (Lens of Sutton)

Part of the original Wolverton & Stony Stratford Tramway track in setts on display at the Milton Keynes Museum of Industry and Rural Life at Wolverton. The tramway closed in May 1926. (Author)

Board of Trade sanction for services to commence was given on 20th May 1887. The line was mostly single and it was built to the 3 ft 6 in gauge and not the 4 ft gauge originally authorised. Public passenger traffic began a week later on 27th May between the Barley Mow Inn at Stony Stratford and Wolverton railway station to connect with all up and down trains and also at times to suit local workers. Initially two steam tram-engines supplied by Krauss of Munich hauled large covered-top double-deck passenger cars obtained from the Midland Carriage and Wagon Co of Shrewsbury.

Two months after opening, an extension of 2 miles 3 chains from Stony Stratford's High Street to Deanshanger was agreed. Work went ahead immediately and a line running almost parallel to the Grand Junction Canal opened later that year. It was hoped that this extension, a private scheme of Wilkinson's leased to the company, would encourage considerable freight traffic from the Britannia Ironworks of E & H Roberts at Deanshanger and in anticipation Wilkinson acquired another Krauss tram-engine and numerous wagons. Two of these were particularly versatile having retractable flanges which allowed horse-drawn road haulage where no track existed. A small 4-wheeled coach was also purchased to cater for the occasional passenger traffic. Unhappily for Wilkinson, the ironworks kept its trade with the canal carriers who had previously brought it considerable business.

In March 1888 a contract was agreed with the LNWR for delivery of goods from Wolverton. Despite this by mid-1889 the company ran into serious financial problems and on 4th September it declared itself insolvent and went into voluntary liquidation. This was contested by various creditors but a Court Order on 26th October closed the line. For about two years the local people had no trams and it was not until 1891 that a local benefactor, Herbert Samuel Leon, of Bletchley Park joined with the local Field family to rescue the company. After negotiations with the Receiver, a

The remains of the bottom half of Wolverton & Stony Stratford tramcar no 5 at the Wolverton Museum – the top half is preserved under cover in the steel barn. Car no 5 was found in Cowpen Wood at Thornton, near Buckingham, where it had served as a game-keeper's hut. (Author)

public service was reinstated on 20th November 1891. This was a purely private arrangement which lasted until September 1893 when yet another tramway company with an even longer title, the Wolverton and Stony Stratford and District New Tramway Company Limited, was formed, controlled by the Leon and Field families.

The Deanshanger extension was no longer in use and the Stony Stratford terminus was cut back to the Cock Inn. The carriage of freight was confined mainly to LNWR parcel traffic and the handling of mail for the Postmaster General. A small store building to handle parcel traffic was established near the gate of the depot at Stony Stratford and a small office and waiting room opened at the corner of High Street and Wolverton Road next door to the Foresters Arms. By this time the earlier Krauss tram-engines had been replaced by engines from T Green & Sons with the Krauss no 3 kept as stand-by.

In 1900 a further tram-engine was purchased from the Brush Electrical Company but it was hardly a satisfactory acquisition. Its cylinders were smaller than the Krauss engines and it could just about haul a workmen's tram. It continually broke down necessitating expensive and difficult repairs. It was perhaps the passenger cars that aroused the most interest. To carry the workers there were three large double-deck cars, each on two 4-wheel bogies and capable of seating 100 passengers. The cars were 44 ft long and each had as many as 16 windows on either side. Interior illumination after dark was from oil-lamps although these were later replaced by the LNWR with acetylene lights. Further cars available carried fewer numbers and these were generally used for passengers other than workmen. In later years the larger cars developed a visible sag in the centre because of the numbers carried although the cars were eventually overhauled and strengthened.

In 1910 economies and increasing motor traffic caused the High

Street section to be abandoned and the trams found a new terminus outside the Foresters Arms in the Wolverton Road. Not surprisingly the presence of 44 ft long cars in formation created problems for other road vehicles. The trams received their first direct competition in 1914 when motor buses from Bedford extended their service to Stony Stratford. Relief came for the trams when war was declared and the whole of the Bedford fleet was requisitioned by the War Office. As the war progressed so maintenance of the tramway system became increasingly difficult. Costs outstripped revenue and in 1916 a motorbus was introduced to help maintain a regular timetable. By the end of the war in 1918 the condition of the tramway was described as 'little better than derelict'.

As a result the company went into liquidation on 17th July 1919 and matters were worsened when the local authorities refused to become involved. Since 700 workers were still being carried daily, the LNWR stepped in and at the end of 1919 purchased the entire undertaking – a move it was soon to regret. A small saddle-tank locomotive was purchased from W & G Bagnall & Co and the tramway was completely re-laid with concrete placed beneath the rails. Meantime by the spring of 1920 motor buses from Bedford were providing a half-hourly service through Stony Stratford and the trams, with their 8 mph speed limit, continued to lose money. The London, Midland & Scottish Railway Company, which took over the LNWR in 1923, struggled on with the trams almost deserted. On 4th May 1926, during the General Strike, services were suspended never to be resumed.

Numerous items from the Wolverton & Stony Stratford Tramway can be studied today at the Milton Keynes Museum of Industry and Rural Life in Wolverton (open between Easter and the end of October, Wednesday to Sunday). Transport is a strong theme with museum exhibits ranging from tram tickets to parts of the original tramcars. The bottom half of no 5 tramcar has been preserved as well as the top and bottom half of a smaller car although, as might be expected, they are in poor condition. In addition copies of original drawings from Wolverton Works are still in existence. Iron track measures and tramcar seats are also displayed, plus parts of the original track in setts, as it would have been when originally laid.

Chapter 10

SINGLE TRACK TO AYLESBURY

(Cheddington to Aylesbury)

Shortly before 5 pm on Saturday, 31st January 1953, the 'Cheddington Flyer' pulled into Aylesbury High Street station. Eager passengers scrambled across the platform in their anxiety to obtain seats and, almost before the train had come to a halt, most of the seats were taken. For the special occasion, the last passenger train along the branch had its number of coaches increased from two to four. One enthusiast hung a Union Jack from a carriage window while others simply sat back and let their minds wander over the earlier days of the 'Flyer'.

The driver, Victor Bunn, and his mate, W Hodgson, obligingly posed in their cab for photographers and then it was time to go. The honour of flagging the train out went to George Thorne who for just over 40 years had served the line. As the train left the station, detonators exploded and there was a mild outburst of cheering and waving as the engine, an ex-LNWR Webb 2–4–2T no 46601, equipped with a klaxon horn, tooted its last farewell. The *Bucks Herald* wrote nostalgically of the occasion, 'The Flyer was being cast aside as one of the things we can do without in this modern age'.

The main line at Cheddington dates back to the 1820s when Robert Stephenson was compelled by opposition from local land-owners to select a route from London to Birmingham to the east of Aylesbury. As a result a meeting was held at the town's White Hart Inn on 10th November 1835 to discuss the possibility of a rail link. There was much support and it was Sir Harry Verney, a local dignitary, who helped the Aylesbury Railway obtain its Act on 19th

A branch from Aylesbury opened in June 1839 to join the London & Birmingham Railway (later LNWR) at Cheddington. In this picture taken in 1912, a squadron of Lancers passes the High Street station courtyard. (Lens of Sutton)

May 1836. Work on the branch was delayed because of an aborted proposal to build a line from Cheltenham via Aylesbury. Eventually the first sod was cut on 12th May 1838 and work went ahead.

When the grand opening came on 10th June 1839, it was a great day for Aylesbury. Shops were closed and local folk were given a whole day's holiday. The first official train left at 7 am, when five first class and three second class carriages were hauled from Aylesbury to Cheddington over the seven miles in 14 minutes. Throughout the day thousands of people thronged the small platform and each departure was to the accompaniment of the Long Crendon village band. To celebrate the occasion, a private banquet was held at the White Hart with tickets at 10 shillings (50p) each. The chairman of the company, George Carrington, told guests that, whereas previously London had been reached by coach taking many hours, the journey could now be undertaken by train in under two hours. Probably the very first rural branch line, it was single track and largely straight, with few earthworks, no tunnels and just one footbridge (at Aylesbury).

Initially there were three trains on each weekday and two on Sunday, all connecting with the London trains at Cheddington. Services were operated from the outset by locomotives and coaches from the London & Birmingham Railway (L&BR). Two small Bury 2–2–0 locomotives were used which were named *Aylesbury no 1* and *Aylesbury no 2*. The station at Aylesbury aroused much interest in Whishaw's *Railways of Great Britain & Ireland* (1842) stating 'the station is conveniently laid out ... the booking office and general waiting room are in one; there is however, a separate room for ladies. This is, upon the whole, one of the best arranged stations for a short line railway that we have anywhere met with'.

During the first years of its life the Aylesbury Railway's future was uncertain. Plans that it should be absorbed by rival companies came to nothing as various proposals failed. Eventually the L&BR took it under an Act obtained on 16th July 1846. At the same time the L&BR became the London & North Western Railway

(LNWR) following amalgamation with the Manchester & Birmingham and the Grand Junction railway companies. In 1851 the LNWR revived an earlier plan to connect Tring with Oxford via the Aylesbury Railway and Thame, presumably to link with the Oxford, Worcester & Wolverhampton Railway. Although approved by the House of Commons, the project was rejected by the House of Lords. It had been proposed the line would cross the Aylesbury branch close to Marston Gate level crossing, where later the only intermediate station was opened. In any event, the plan was poorly received by the Aylesbury residents who were not at all happy about the prospect of a level crossing in their High Street.

1851 was also the year of the Great Exhibition which took place within the Crystal Palace, built in London's Hyde Park. This huge expanse of iron and glass, somewhat like a greenhouse and designed by (Sir) Joseph Paxton was later re-erected at Sydenham in south London but it was accidentally destroyed by fire in 1936. (The author vividly recalls the spectacular inferno visible for miles around). Aylesbury's interest came in July, when a rail excursion to the Great Exhibition catered for around a thousand people transported in thirty carriages. The small station must surely have been hard-pushed to cope with such numbers.

During the following year an incident took place which proved the usefulness of the new electric telegraph already installed on the main line. A robbery took place in Aylesbury and the thief used the branch line to make his escape. The police, knowing of his movements, made urgently for Tring station where the electric telegraph was used to contact Euston. When the train arrived the thief was duly arrested. The device was installed at Aylesbury station on 23rd July 1859 when the local press loudly acclaimed

Ex-LNWR Webb 2-4-2T no 46601 (LMS class 1P) built 1890, seen at Aylesbury High Street station on 31st January 1953 awaiting departure. (John H Meredith)

'Aylesbury was now in communication with London – indeed all the world'.

In 1863 the Aylesbury branch's monopoly came to an end when a broad gauge line reached the town from Princes Risborough. This was a Wycombe Railway attempt (under the auspices of the GWR) to capture London traffic by offering a more direct route rather than north-eastwards via Cheddington. Some five years later, in September 1868, trains reached Aylesbury from Verney Junction and, within a few weeks, conversion of the Princes Risborough line to standard gauge was completed. In anticipation of these events, there had been pressure on the railway companies to provide Aylesbury with a single railway station, particularly bearing in mind the LNWR terminus which was now considered quite inadequate. The petition failed partly because a particular property (the Bear Inn) on a proposed link line had not previously been purchased for demolition.

On 12th July 1883, the branch line received a Royal visit. In his book, *The Aylesbury Railway*, Bill Simpson wrote that when King Edward VII was Prince of Wales, he visited the LNWR Aylesbury

Marston Gate crossing and station looking in the Aylesbury direction, photographed after closure of passenger services in 1953 and after removal of the station signs showing the original lettering underneath. (Lens of Sutton)

An LNWR 4-4-0 locomotive (known as the 'Jubilee' class) at Cheddington station c1910. The branch platform for the seven-mile long single-track branch to Aylesbury is on the right. (Lens of Sutton)

station en route to Waddesdon Manor (on the line to Verney Junction and still under construction). Unfortunately the LNWR made little effort to decorate the station although everything was presented 'in a neat and polished condition'. However, the townsfolk made up for any omission with a generous display of bunting, streamers and placards to welcome the Prince. Perhaps the highlight of the event was the generosity of the gas company which made available 10,000 cu ft of gas free to illuminate the decorations by night.

Aylesbury station greatly improved when, faced with the threat of increased competition, a more conveniently sited building opened on 16th June 1889 fronting on to the High Street. The Metropolitan Railway had already reached as far north as Chesham and plans were well in hand to reach Aylesbury. The new station was built in brick with its single platform under a glass canopy. The number of staff compared favourably with any station of today including a stationmaster, four porters, five clerks, three carters and two signalmen! Freight too was an important commodity and, with the Dominion Dairy close to the station, considerable quantities of the company's well known Golden Acre butter, were transported along the branch. In addition barley and hops were carried to the Aylesbury Brewery with beer later returning to Cheddingon in large vats on flat wagons. The town also gained fame with its printing firm of Hazell, Watson & Viney which, apart from many well known magazines, produced and exported copies of the Reader's Digest magazine.

When the joint Metropolitan and GWR station opened on 1st January 1894, the LNWR branch lost much of its importance and the branch could no longer effectively compete for London traffic. During the First World War it was used to carry vast quantities of tinned foods especially for consumption by the armed forces. The English Condensed Milk Company opened in Aylesbury in 1870 to eventually become the well known Nestle Company producing large amounts of condensed milk. Many will recall the station chocolate machines which carried Nestle products.

During the 1920s the branch became part of the London, Midland & Scottish Railway (LMS). The line, like many in the area, had its share of problems during the Second World War. A bomb exploding near Marston Gate station made many reluctant to travel by rail and on another occasion the engine shed at Aylesbury was damaged by a landmine. Nationalisation came in 1948, yet the line lingered on. Finally, on 31st January 1953, the final passenger train left Aylesbury for Cheddington. Freight traffic survived another ten years, much of the traffic being agricultural and livestock plus much business from printers, Hazell, Watson & Viney. While the station building became a store used by a local wine and spirit company, freight locomotives seen along the line included Stanier class 5s and 8Fs, as well as ex-LNWR 0–8–0s and Ivatt class tank engines. The branch closed completely on 2nd December 1963.

Class 2 2-6-2T no 41275 (designed by Ivatt and built at Crewe 1950 to LMS design) with coaches waits at Cheddington on the Aylesbury branch on 31st January 1953. (John H Meredith)

The main line just north of Cheddington became famous earlier that year on 8th August 1963 when train robbers daringly held up the Royal Mail train at Bridego Bridge to steal 120 bags containing some £2,600,000 which they then transported to nearby Leatherslade Farm. This became known of course as 'The Great Train Robbery' which achieved considerable publicity. Sadly train driver Jack Mills suffered ill-health for many years after the event following the brutal beating he had received and he died in 1970. At the trial of the robbers held at Aylesbury, sentences reaching 30 years imprisonment were handed out although one of the men had got away – to live in hiding. He was Ronald Biggs, a name surely still recalled by many today. One may wonder if the robbers considered the hold-up really worth while – it would seem the only people to really profit were those who made a film of the episode several years later.

The Aylesbury branch line is still remembered with affection by many local folk. The drivers knew many of the passengers and often checked all were there each morning. If anyone arrived late, they would stop the train and hoist the late-comer up into the carriage. It was a truly rural line. Sometimes a train could be delayed because cattle had strayed onto the track and had to be driven off. When the author visited Aylesbury in May 1991, the High Street station area had been cleared, ready for a 'Spring 1992 Inner Relief Road development'. The approach road was still there, blocked by sleepers, and one building remained to recall the past. It was an office, 'W J Hawkins Ltd., Coal Merchants'. At Cheddington the bay could be determined but work was in hand to remove the platform edges.

Bridego Bridge, near Cheddington, May 1991, where 28 years previously the 'Great Train Robbery' took place and when 120 bags containing some £2,600,000 were stolen. (Author)

The wooden station building at Marston Gate had long since been replaced by a fine private residence. It was possible to ascertain where the track had crossed, and the pillar box at the site read 'Marston Gate'. Perhaps recollections of the station can best be expressed by this excerpt from 'Marston Gate' by local poet Christine Dunker:

> There really was a station – Marston Gate –
> With early morning gloom if train was late
> When passengers would huddle round the fire;
> No morning papers, nothing to inspire
>
> The roving eyes, save battered wooden clock
> Precisely stating time with tick and tock
> Until the noise was drowned by piercing scream
> As train arrived with hissing spouting steam.
>
> A sudden rush, no waste of precious time,
> The doors flung wide, and high athletic climb
> To smoke-filled carriage, dimly dark and grey,
> With corner seat, and crumbs of yesterday.

Chapter 11

THE 'NICKY LINE' TO HARPENDEN

(Hemel Hempstead to Harpenden)

The line that began as the Hemel Hempstead Railway was unique since it was the only Midland Railway branch in Hertfordshire. It was also unusual because, although the single track of just under nine miles linked Harpenden with the busy market town of Hemel Hempstead (originally spelled Hemel Hempsted), passenger services never reached the main LNWR line from Euston. Many considered the line was charmingly eccentric, sometimes operated with a loaned 4–4–0T locomotive pulling a rather elderly first class Pullman car available with third class fares.

Today's BR Hemel Hempstead station was originally known as Boxmoor and it assumed historic importance when from 20th July 1837 for nearly three months it was the temporary terminus of the London & Birmingham Railway (LNWR from 1846) while Stephenson carried on up the valley towards Tring. This left Hemel Hempstead town marooned on its hill to the east so various proposals followed to connect the two areas. The Hemel Hempstead Railway succeeded by an Act of 1863 with an authorised capital of £20,000 and £6,600 on loan. As a result of this, a line was laid from the LNWR goods yard across Boxmoor to Cotterells

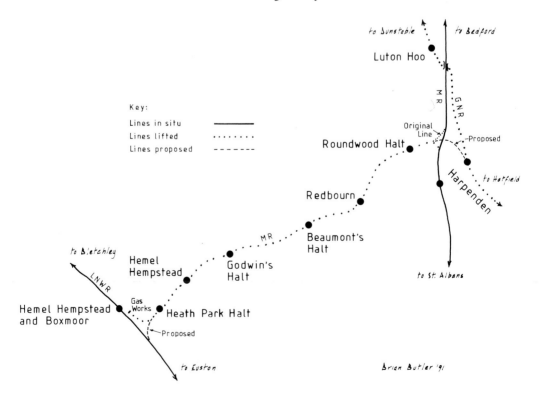

An ex M&GN 4-4-0T (built 1879) on loan to the Midland Railway plus Pullman car, converted to become a 'push-pull' motor train, at Heath Park Halt c1910 on the Hemel Hempstead to Harpenden branch line. (Lens of Sutton)

near Heath Park where later a depot followed. It had been intended that passenger traffic as well as goods would use the line although, when constructed, the only physical link with the LNWR was by turntable.

The short section was never used, probably because of difficulties with the Boxmoor Trust, wealthy owners of the protected common known as Boxmoor. A further Act in 1866 agreed the line should be abandoned although the rails were not removed. Instead a new route was planned from Hemel Hempstead to Harpenden connecting at the latter end with the Great Northern Railway's

The site of Heath Park Halt in May 1991, almost 45 years after the line closed to passengers. Boxmoor House on the left has become an Arts Centre while Heath Park Hotel has been rebuilt. Far left, behind the tree, can just be determined the Kodak Hemel Hempstead centre. (Author)

Hemel Hempstead station c1910. The single line branch of almost 9 miles opened for passenger traffic on 16th July 1877. On the first day free rides were available for all. (Lens of Sutton)

(GNR) Hertford, Luton & Dunstable branch as well as the London extension of the Midland Railway. Parliament approved the proposal in 1866 authorising an increase in capital to £170,000 plus £56,600 on loan. Construction from Heath Park towards Harpenden began the same year.

The Hemel Hempstead Railway had still not given up the idea of connecting with the LNWR at Boxmoor but relations between the two companies were so poor that no such link developed. It is thought that the Midland Railway feared a diversion over LNWR lines of through-London traffic which would otherwise have to take the longer journey over its own branch via Harpenden. It is also considered possible the Boxmoor Trust was not in favour since it collected tolls in the area. Instead, under an Act of 1872, powers were given to re-open the extension from Cotterells to Boxmoor goods station and some freight traffic developed.

When the branch opened on 16th July 1877, there were free first-day rides for everyone. Nothing further was heard of the proposed connection with the Hertford, Luton & Dunstable line so a north-facing junction linked the branch with the Midland Luton station while passengers for London could change at Chiltern Green. Hemel Hempstead was an important source of raw material from reed beds for the straw hat industry and its links at that time were therefore greater with Luton than with London. There were three trains each way daily and the total journey of 13¼ miles between Hemel Hempstead and Luton took about 40 minutes. Traffic suffered however when London-bound passengers from Hemel Hempstead found it quicker to travel via Boxmoor reaching the station by an LNWR horse-bus. Consideration was given to a south-facing link since it was considered that Harpenden was a more suitable junction station but it was not until 1888, two years after absorption of the company by the Midland Railway, that this was completed. The original north-facing route was abandoned and trains now ran into a small bay at Harpenden beside the down fast platform.

Following the Midland Railway take-over, services were increased to seven trains each way daily (with no Sunday service) with connections for St Pancras reaching London in a little more than one hour. Another service available was a through afternoon service from Hemel Hempstead to St Albans and back which continued to run until 1895. The earliest locomotives to work the line were three George England 2–4–0 tender engines transferred from the Somerset & Dorset Joint Railway with the numbers 9, 10 and 13 becoming 1397, 1398 and 1399. Near the Harpenden end of the line there was a steep incline of 1 in 37 which sometimes proved too much for overloaded engines which meant that loads had to be strictly limited.

In 1905 the Midland introduced a rail-motor push-pull service and it was shortly afterwards that the ex-Eastern & Midlands 4–4–0T and the elderly Pullman parlour coach were introduced. After this the line was generally operated by 0–4–4T and 0–6–0T engines. At first the only intermediate branch station was at Redbourn but on 9th August 1906 trains were extended from Hemel Hempstead to Heath Park Halt making the branch one of the very few to have a halt for a terminus. On the same day, to encourage local traffic, further halts were opened at Beaumont's and Godwin's and the service was further increased to nine trips daily. Roundwood halt came later on 8th August 1927.

In 1912 the 4–4–0Ts were returned to the Midland & Great Northern Joint Railway and the place of the Pullman was taken by a steam motor carriage which had become redundant following electrification of the Lancaster–Morecambe–Heysham line. The Hemel Hempstead branch became part of the London, Midland & Scottish Railway (LMS) in 1923 which introduced an alternative bus service in 1929. This reduced train services to peak times only so that just one locomotive was needed. The buses at last connected Hemel Hempstead and Boxmoor and rail tickets could be used. In 1931 there was an experiment when a road-rail bus was introduced. The vehicle, built by the Karrier Motor Company of Huddersfield, ran principally between Hemel Hempstead and Redbourn and could travel on roads or rails by lifting and lowering the road wheels or flanged wheels as needful. Change-over ramps were provided at various points along the line. In 1933 the London Passenger Transport Board (LPTB) took over the LMSR bus undertakings and abandoned the project before the experiment could justify itself. A similar vehicle was later used successfully on the Stratford-on-Avon & Midland Junction Railway.

A reduced service survived the 1939–1945 war but passenger trains finally ceased on 16th June 1947 during a coal crisis. Freight continued for a number of years and there was opportunity in the 1950s when Hemel Hempstead was selected as a post-war 'New Town' development area. A modern freight terminal was planned at Godwin's Halt but unfortunately BR and the Hemel Hempstead Development Corporation could not agree on the railway's role and the chance was lost. The branch gradually declined with the

The down platform at Harpenden on the Thameslink line in May 1991. The bay platform that served Hemel Hempstead trains has long since gone. The original Midland platform building was destroyed by fire in the early 1970s with today's rebuilt to the same style. (Author)

Boxmoor Gas Works section including Cotterells Yard being the first to go. Access to the gasworks was maintained by finally opening a physical link with the former LNWR goods yard but within a few weeks the gas works closed and the line was hardly used. Meantime rail enthusiasts had an opportunity to travel the branch when on 10th August 1958 a Railway Correspondence & Travel Society tour hauled by 3F 0–6–0 no 43245 covered the tracks one last time.

Hemel Hempstead goods yard closed from 1st July 1963 followed by Godwin's Depot on 2nd March 1964. For a time the line became truncated at the siding of the Claydale Brick & Tile Company, six miles from Harpenden, but when electrification came to the 'Midland' main line in June 1979, the branch was finally severed. The track to Claydale was lifted in 1982 after which time much of the branch trackbed became a walkway – known appropriately as the 'Nicky Walk'. A number of the diesel locomotives that served the branch survived. D2207 class 3 built in 1953 went to the North Yorkshire Moors Railway together with D8568, the sole survivor in its class. D2203 was sold in 1981 to later reach the Yorkshire Dales Railway at Embsay.

Although passenger services ceased almost 45 years ago, the line is still recalled with affection by many. Some residents remember that the branch's reputation for punctuality was such that 'watches and clocks could be set by the train'. It was claimed the train became so reliable that some called her 'Faithful Annie'. Yet to those who today think they still hear the whistle of a steam engine near Hemel Hempstead's town centre, it has become 'The Ghost of Puffing Annie'.

Chapter 12

A LINE FROM AN ABBEY

(St Albans to Hatfield)

Over the centuries St Albans has seen many battles. As long ago as AD 43 Roman armies occupied what had originally been a Belgic settlement, named it *Verulamium*, and made it one of the most important towns in their Western Empire. In about AD 209 Alban, a Romano British citizen, was beheaded for his faith on a nearby hilltop to become Britain's first Christian martyr. Here the abbey, which replaced the small Saxon church built on his shrine, developed into a magnificent cathedral. Yet the visitor to St Albans today would no doubt be surprised to learn that evidence from more recent battles could be found in an open space only half a mile from the abbey grounds.

Whilst walking in undergrowth just below the London Road, the author found two Sherman tanks – one in good working condition – and other vehicles including army scout cars. But these were not relics from a battle on the site but the private collection of a scrap metal merchant, whose many items stand in the former yard of St Albans London Road railway station. In the adjacent goods yard, beyond where a cattle pen once existed, could be found a derelict goods shed. Through the nearby bushes, guns from army vehicles pointed at non-existent targets. . . .

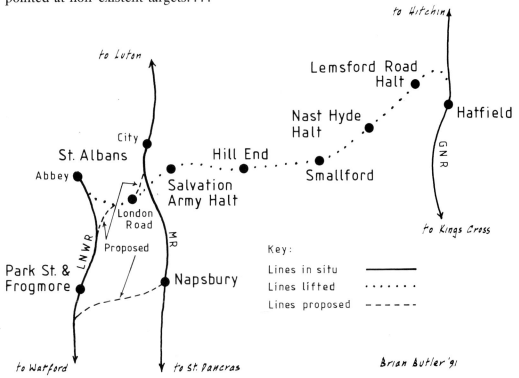

Brian Butler '91

Prior to the London & North Western Railway (LNWR) opening a branch from St Albans to Watford in 1858, the city's only rail link with London was by coach to Hatfield and then by Great Northern Railway (GNR) to King's Cross. Earlier in 1847 the LNWR had obtained Parliamentary approval to construct a loop between Watford and Leighton Buzzard passing through St Albans and Redbourn but this failed to materialise. When the LNWR opened its 6½ mile single track branch from St Albans to Watford, the GNR saw this as a clear threat to its Hatfield traffic. Four years later, on 30th June 1862, authority was granted for a line to be built from St Albans to Hatfield. There was difficulty in raising finance but, with GNR support, the Hatfield & St Albans Railway Company went ahead with construction of the line.

There was concern in 1863 when the Midland Railway (MR) obtained powers to build a line from Bedford to St Pancras which would pass through St Albans offering a quicker and more direct route to London than either of the two branches. The proposal was not to compete with the GNR or LNWR but a need for the MR, a northern company serving many coalfields, to have access to the London markets. MR trains were already reaching Hitchin from Leicester but the final stretch to King's Cross could only be made over GNR lines. Unfortunately the GNR often gave preference to its own services and on one occasion a queue of waiting MR trains reached a length of five miles. In 1868 the MR completed its own direct (and only) line, via St Albans, into London.

Nevertheless the branch from St Albans to Hatfield went ahead, probably unwisely, opening on 16th October 1865. One intermediate station was planned at Springfield (renamed Smallford in 1879)

A British United Traction 3-car multiple unit set at St Albans Abbey station used on the Watford branch in the 1950s. These cars were disliked by many passengers who complained of 'rough riding and ineffective heating' so the line reverted to steam during the winter 1955/56. (Lens of Sutton)

but it was not ready in time for the line's opening. The Act gave the GNR (which worked the line) running powers into the LNWR's St Albans station. Travelling the line, this was reached after negotiating a curve from St Albans' London Road station with GNR trains terminating in a bay on the eastern side of the single platform. Opposite there were extensive sidings leading to St Albans gasworks (which has long since gone) with both GNR and LNWR trains bringing coal to the plant. According to the *Hertford Mercury*, there were initially eight trains daily in each direction and two on Sundays. Passenger coaches were four-wheeled vehicles, lit by oil lamps and it was not until 1883 that gas-lit coaches were introduced. The coaches were probably hauled by Sharp 2–2–2Ts and the branch journey took 15 minutes. The single fare from St Albans to King's Cross was 3/6d (17½p) first class, 2/6d (12½p) second class and 1/11½d (just under 10p) third class. If a passenger took a horse with him it cost an extra 5/– (25p) and a dog 1/– (5p). On weekdays, trains went through to the LNWR (Abbey) station but on Sundays the two passenger trains terminated at London Road.

When the MR station opened, receipts on the branch fell and debts could not be paid. In 1870 a Receiver was appointed and the independent company had little choice but to become absorbed by the GNR. This was formalised by an Act of Parliament on 1st November 1883. Debts were paid off, shareholders received 23% of the face value of their shares and the Hatfield & St Albans Railway Company no longer existed. The branch continued under its new ownership although hopes to build up London traffic were frustrated by the MR's new line, with the GNR continuing to run at a loss. To encourage traffic a few through coaches ran from St Albans to King's Cross but these did not survive long. Cheap excursions were arranged which included a holiday of up to six days in Scarborough for a return rail fare of 7/6d (37½p). Similarly passengers could travel to King's Cross in 1893 for 1/9d (less than 9p) third class return to attend such outings as a Brewery Exhibition at the Royal Agricultural Hall, 'Niagara Falls in Winter'

Ex-LMS 0-4-4T Stanier class 2P no 41901 heads a Railway Correspondence & Travel Society tour on 27th April 1958 reaching St Albans from Watford. (Lens of Sutton)

St Albans London Road station closed to passengers on 1st October 1951 and visitors to the site today might be surprised to find Sherman tanks and other army vehicles. These form part of a private collection of the owner of the site, a scrap metal merchant. (Author)

at Westminster or a Dog Show at the Crystal Palace. The last visit required a further 1/6d (7½p) which also included admission to the show.

In 1899 a further intermediate station opened at Hill End (to serve the Herts County Mental Hospital), followed by Salvation Army Halt where a printing works opened in 1901. The press published such books as *The War Cry* and *Young Soldier*. Nast Hyde Halt followed in 1910. By the late 1930s the number of passengers was declining and when the war came in 1939 the LNER (formerly GNR) withdrew all passenger services. Within three months trains had to restart to meet the needs of the many St Albans people travelling to the De Havilland Aircraft Works at Hatfield. After the war, numbers fell again and on 1st October 1951 the line closed to passengers for good.

The line lingered on into the 1960s with freight traffic serving the many industrial sidings along the branch, during which time special excursions were organised by various societies. The branch saw fame too when stations were used for a number of film and TV productions. Smallford station was used more than once and, more recently, London Road station was used for TV films such as 'The Return of the Saint' and 'The Rivals of Sherlock Holmes'. The trackbed today can be traced mostly as footpaths or cycle tracks and a number of bridges have been retained. The site of Hill End station now provides temporary accommodation for homeless while at Smallford the platform building has become an office to a scrap metal yard. Concrete posts, once the entrance to a goods yard, were in evidence and the platform, cleared a few years ago, has once more been taken over by undergrowth.

In contrast, the single track line from St Albans to Watford, which was electrified in 1988, continues to survive. Commuters use the branch which must surely be unique, with further stations opening in recent years. Garston station opened in 1966 with How Wood station following as recently as July 1988. The rebuilding of

Bricket Wood on the Watford branch in early LMS days. The second platform and crossing loop were added in 1913 to handle increased numbers of excursion trains. (Lens of Sutton)

Bricket Wood station on a wet May morning in 1991 with only one platform surviving and the loop gone. Shuttle services run hourly between St Albans Abbey station and Watford Junction. (Author)

Watford Junction station was completed in 1985. Earlier in the branch's life, a link was proposed from north of Park Street which would have carried trains from Watford briefly onto the Hatfield branch and then a further link onto the Midland line. Also at the time the Midland main line was built in the 1860s, a contractor's line was built from the Watford branch to the MR route at Napsbury. This was later removed but requests have persisted through to recent times for this to be reinstated thus allowing the almost redundant Abbey station to be closed. Although certain of the earthworks still exist, it would seem such a scheme would be impractical on cost grounds alone.

When the author visited St Albans by car, he was stopped outside the town with other traffic at a police survey and asked various questions. The officer asked finally 'Where are you going?' Back came the answer 'London Road railway station'. 'But that's been closed for years . . .' he was replying as the car pulled away. He could still be seen in the car rear-view mirror scratching his head.

Chapter 13

ACROSS TWO COUNTIES

(Hertford to Hatfield/Hatfield to Luton and Dunstable/Dunstable
to Leighton Buzzard)

Hertford to Hatfield

Hertford's greatest claim to fame is surely that its castle is the
oldest building in the county dating back to c1100. Until the reign
of Elizabeth I it was closely connected with royalty and when
Edward III's mother died, he recruited a guard of 14 poor persons
at twopence a day for three months to guard over her body.
Another building of note is Lombard House on Bull Plain, the
17th century home of Henry Chauncy, the Hertfordshire historian
and judge, who presided over one of the last witchcraft trials in
Britain. The railways first reached the town in October 1843 from
Broxbourne and, fifteen years later, an independent branch from
Welwyn reached the town.

  The Hertford & Welwyn Junction Railway, promoted by a group
of London and Hertford businessmen, obtained Parliamentary
approval on 3rd July 1854. The company later amalgamated with
the Luton, Dunstable & Welwyn Junction Railway, to form the
Hertford, Luton & Dunstable Railway (HL&DR) by an Act of
28th June 1858. There had been considerable rivalry between the
Great Northern Railway (GNR) and the Eastern Counties Railway
(GER from 1862) for the Hertford traffic but eventually this was
resolved when the GNR purchased the HL&DR in 1861.

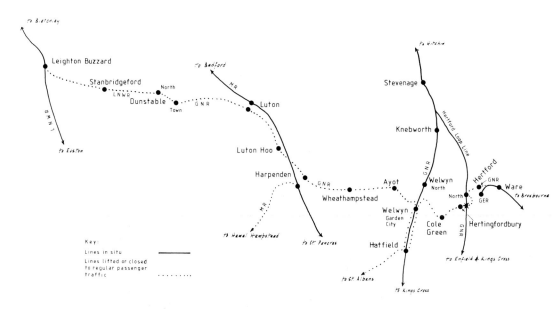

Services began on 1st March 1858 over the nine mile branch with intermediate stations at Hertingfordbury and Cole Green. Locomotives and rolling stock were provided by the GNR and in Hertford a station was opened at Cowbridge, about half a mile west of the Eastern Counties station. Five trains ran each way daily with two on Sundays but since trains were not allowed to cross the main line at Welwyn, the branch was taken southwards to terminate at Hatfield. There was no station at Welwyn and it was not until 1920 that the Hertford branch provided a crude platform where trains stopped by request. It was to be another six years before a more substantial station was built, from which beginnings came the vast industrial area of Welwyn Garden City. The first factory to be built was that of the Shredded Wheat Company which developed a daily run of up to 30 wagons a day. Another pioneer of the day was Frank Murphy who in 1930 with three men founded a wireless factory. Within three years there was an output of 600 radios daily.

Earlier the final stage of the 'Hertford Loop Line' (as it became known) had been completed providing a station at Hertford North. The loop came into existence because the GNR was experiencing serious bottleneck problems on its main line into King's Cross. A branch reached Enfield in 1871 and, rather than bear the costs to widen track and enlarge tunnels on its main line, the GNR gained Parliamentary approval in 1898 to complete a 'bypass' from Enfield to Stevenage. Progress was intermittent with tracks reaching Cuffley in 1910. The loop was completed in 1920 but passenger services did not commence until 2nd June 1924. This made the Hertford & Welwyn station at Cowbridge redundant so it closed to passengers on the same day and branch trains used the new Hertford North station. The route to Cowbridge with a connection through to Hertford East was kept open for freight.

Hertford's GNR station at Cowbridge which closed to passengers on 2nd June 1924. When the Hertford Loop line opened, passengers used the new Hertford North station. (Lens of Sutton)

91

Hertingfordbury on the GNR Hertford to Hatfield branch which closed in June 1951. Freight services survived another 11 years until 1962. (Lens of Sutton)

Cole Green station building and the remains of platforms photographed in the 1960s long after closure to passengers. (Lens of Sutton)

Because branch trains from Hertford or Dunstable were not allowed to cross the main GNR route at Welwyn, services terminated at Hatfield. In this picture, c1910, a GNR 2-4-0 (designed by P Stirling) hauls a passenger set out of Hatfield station. (Lens of Sutton).

Class A4 4-6-2 no 4492 Dominion of New Zealand emerges from Welwyn tunnel in 1937 on the main LNER route northwards to Peterborough and Grantham. (D K Jones)

During the 1939–1945 war, the branch was connected with the up main line at Welwyn and from September 1944 Hertford trains terminated at Welwyn Garden City instead of Hatfield. Passenger services continued from Hatfield to Cole Green, Hertingfordbury and Hertford North until 18th June 1951 when the branch became an early victim to closure. The last train, hauled by class N7 locomotive no 69695, carried many passengers and reached Welwyn Garden City at 7.33 pm. In a last moment of glory, two weeks before closure an LMS-reconstructed Liverpool & Manchester engine and three coaches were used to help make the Anna Neagle film '*Lady with the Lamp*'.

Hatfield to Luton and Dunstable

At 10.33 am on 26th July 1948 a porter spotted a fire at Ayot station (between Wheathampstead and Welwyn) just after a train had left. Two hours later the station was gutted and the track had curled and buckled in the heat. A newspaper report stated, 'During the blaze, smoke and flame enveloped the station and the smell of burning creosote drifted for miles. Firemen struggled across fields with hydrants but the all-wooden structure defeated them; only cinders and a chimney stack remained of the up-platform with its waiting room. Spectators helped the firemen handle a pump and hoses over the burning track and across fields to a nearby pond'. Services were restored during the afternoon but the station was never rebuilt and subsequently closed to passenger traffic on 26th September 1949.

The branch began as the Luton, Dunstable & Welwyn Junction Railway which obtained Parliamentary approval on 16th July 1855. After opening a passenger service between Dunstable and Luton

Luton (Bute Street) station which closed to passengers in April 1965 having served trains to Dunstable or Hatfield. A single track to Dunstable still exists (used by freight) and there is a possibility this may one day carry passengers to Dunstable once again. (Lens of Sutton)

on 3rd May 1858, the company found itself short of funds so an extension beyond Luton was shelved. It was only when the amalgamation with the Hertford & Welwyn Railway took place to form the Hertford, Luton & Dunstable Railway (HL&DR), that further construction could be considered. Even then the work was not carried out on time and a further Act of 21st July 1859 had to be issued to allow completion. A line between Luton and Welwyn eventually opened on 1st September 1860 with intermediate stations at New Mill End (Luton Hoo from 1891), Harpenden, Wheathampstead and Ayott St Peter's (Ayot from 1878). Like the Hertford to Hatfield branch, HL&DR trains could not cross the GNR main line at Welwyn so they terminated at Hatfield. The single-track section of just over 20 miles between Luton and Dunstable was initially worked by the London & North Western Railway (LNWR) but when Hatfield was reached, the GNR took over the whole line. On 12th June 1861, because of HL&DR deficits not cleared, the GNR, aware of the importance of the line, absorbed the company completely.

When services began in 1858 there were five trains each way daily on weekdays only, with two of these later going through to Leighton Buzzard. From September 1860, a Sunday service began between Dunstable Church Street (Dunstable Town from 1927) and Hatfield. Since there were no reversing facilities at Dunstable, a complicated method had to be devised. After passengers had alighted, the train reversed back towards Luton up a slight incline. The guard then applied the brake whereupon the engine was uncoupled and run into a siding. On hearing a whistle from the engine, the guard released the brake and the coaches ran back into the station. The engine could then be correctly placed for its journey back to Hatfield.

By the late 1880s there were eight trains each way daily but still only two on Sundays. In addition there were excursions and one of these organised for Easter Monday 1886 carried 300 passengers to Hyde Park's Crystal Palace. Many of these special services left at a very early hour (one for Llandudno departed at 4.40 am!) and in the book *The Hatfield, Luton & Dunstable Railway*, G & S Woodward gave an account of a Luton gentleman who wanted to make sure he was ready on time. Determined not to miss the train, he decided to sit up all night dressed and at the ready, bowler hat in hand. Unfortunately when the time came he was fast asleep and, living close to the line at Luton Hoo, he awoke in time to hear his train leaving.

Passenger traffic increased satisfactorily over the years that followed. Even though the Midland Railway (MR) had reached Luton offering a more direct route to and from London, it did not always offer a better service. Many MR trains stopped at all stations so passengers often chose express trains from Hatfield to King's Cross with certain trains providing a through service from Dunstable. It was suggested that one particular train, the 7 pm to Hatfield, was reliably punctual since it frequently carried the Prime Minister, Lord Salisbury! In 1906 George Bernard Shaw moved to Ayot St Lawrence to become another important passenger. Unfortunately for station staff, he often arrived late leaving his chauffeur to go on ahead holding up the train until he arrived.

Luton, being the largest town on the route, became an important freight centre with a large coal yard built in 1906 to the south of Luton Bute Street station. Luton was also the centre of the hat industry with consignments received and despatched by rail. Large warehouses were built and in the evenings the area would be congested with hat boxes destined for markets in many places. Freight wagons carrying hats left each evening for King's Cross or the North of England and on one occasion, due to a backlog of loading, a despatch of 756 boxes left Luton as late as 1.50 am. Wheathampstead also carried its share of goods traffic. Being an agricultural area, the railway was often used for transporting

Dunstable's former GNR Church Street station (renamed Dunstable Town in 1927), c1910. The station closed to passengers in April 1965 and the site has been subsequently demolished. (Lens of Sutton)

Dunstable's LNWR station (Dunstable North from 1950). The locomotive appears to be ex-LNWR 0-6-2T with a push-pull train c1930. (Lens of Sutton)

animals and local nurseries despatched large quantities of fresh salad. A commodity often imported into the station yard was manure from the London Zoo although residents in Rose Lane opposite the sidings were not so happy about this.

By the 1930s traffic declined with passengers lost to good local bus services but freight remained active for a number of years. Luton prospered when the Vauxhall motor industry came to the town, but when it stopped sending export vehicles by rail, branch freight declined. In addition Vauxhall Motors no longer had a need for coal and nurseries along the branch were also disappearing. Following the abolition of steam working, three-unit Metro-Cammell railcars took over much of the passenger working. When closure of the line was threatened for 6th January 1965 under the 'Beeching Axe', there were many objections and a reprieve was obtained. Unhappily it was only a brief one and the line finally closed to passengers on 26th April 1965. The last train carrying a nameplate 'The Last Skimpot Flyer' (the nick-name Skimpot referred to a farm along the route) was hauled by a diesel type 1 no D8046. It left Luton Bute Street at 7.55 pm for Welwyn to a quiet farewell with only small groups of onlookers along the line. The secretary of the Bedfordshire and Hertfordshire Passenger Association, which had fought hard to block the closure, said, 'We shall not disband. This is not the end of the fight. Perhaps one day the line might be re-opened'.

Although track between Welwyn and Luton was later ripped up, the single line between Luton and Dunstable remained in existence giving cement and oil trains access to private sidings at Dunstable. Because of this, speculation has continued to the present time over the possibility of restoring a public transport service. Plans for a light railway using single-coach railbuses during peak hours have been put forward with local backing. British Rail in February 1989 said that if a rail link went ahead then electric trains would be favoured giving a possible full service between Dunstable, Luton and London. In early 1991 transport chiefs were considering conversion of the disused line into a bus-only road but this caused concern in Dunstable where people thought the rail link might be lost for ever. A further view expressed foresaw a tramway system giving an 11-station line to also include Luton Airport. A final decision has still to be made, a factor very much dependent upon the availability of finance.

Visiting the former HL&DR line, it is possible to find many reminders of the past. Part of the trackbed around Ayot (apart from that lost to the A1M motorway) has become a nature trail known as the 'Ayot Greenway'. Looking for traces of Ayot station (the building burnt down in 1948), the author found in the under-growth signalling equipment carrying the name 'Saxby & Farmer, London'. At Luton Bute Street the station has gone but the goods shed remains. At the approach road where once hat boxes were loaded on drays, the awning is still there and recent road repair revealed evidence of railway track beneath the surface. Nearby the former engine shed has retained its 'steam escape hole' in the middle of the building.

Dunstable to Leighton Buzzard

Unlike the HL&DR, The Dunstable Railway from Leighton Buzzard was worked throughout by the LNWR. It was agreed by an Act of 1845 and opened for goods traffic on 29th May 1848. Passenger services followed on 1st June 1848, the first to reach Dunstable and ten years prior to the arrival of trains from Luton. The seven mile branch was double track and its only intermediate station was at Stanbridgeford which opened to passengers in 1849 although the platforms were not completed until 1860. Leighton Buzzard station (known as Leighton until 1911) opened earlier in April 1838 during Stephenson's push northwards to link London and Birmingham.

Stanbridgeford station looking towards Dunstable in the early 1960s. Earlier the station had handled a fair amount of goods traffic, mainly cattle. (Lens of Sutton)

Earlier the London & Birmingham Railway (LNWR from 1846) had intended to build a loop line to link Leighton Buzzard with Dunstable, an area of local importance which included sand workings and quarried stone, but this had not come about. Instead the short branch was constructed and there appeared no doubt that Stephenson also looked towards Luton. This latter proposal was rejected by the people of Luton and it was not until 1858 that the GNR reached the town.

When the Leighton Buzzard to Dunstable section opened there were seven trains daily in each direction. There were no Sunday services because of a restriction imposed by a landowner over whose land much of the branch ran. Freight traffic was comparatively light although there were useful quantities of coal delivered to Dunstable Gas Works and chalk was collected from Totternhoe. Stanbridgeford goods traffic was mainly cattle although a market gardener from Eaton Bray sent strawberries and carnations by rail. At Leighton Buzzard there was much activity at Grovebury Sidings where sand was brought in from the nearby sandpits (see chapter 14).

When the Welwyn trains reached their terminus at Dunstable Church Street in 1860, the GNR (which now owned the Welwyn company) sought a means to link with the Leighton Buzzard LNWR branch. Parliament refused permission for a level crossing so a bridge had to be built which gave the GNR access to the LNWR line, just west of the LNWR Watling Street terminus. To overcome this problem, the LNWR requested that the GNR should build a new station and the GNR in return offered to rebuild Church Street. The LNWR agreed provided it had equal rights to the GNR station but the GNR rejected this immediately. Despite the differences, GNR trains were allowed to use the LNWR station by reversing into it. Eventually, after all negotiations had failed, the LNWR built a new station at Dunstable North which opened in 1866.

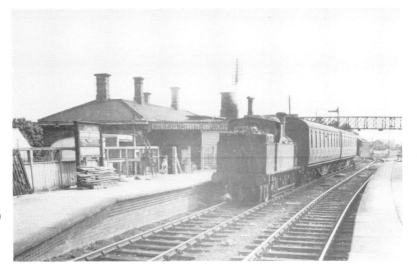

Ex-LNWR 0-6-2T (designed by F W Webb and known as 'coal tanks') at Leighton Buzzard station in the 1950s. (Lens of Sutton)

Leighton Buzzard station, May 1991, undergoing a rebuild programme. A 321 class train waits to depart – Dunstable trains used to leave from a bay beyond the platform on the left. (Author)

Like the Welwyn branch, the Leighton Buzzard to Dunstable line failed to attract any important traffic. Yet excursions were many, including regular football specials for Luton Town's home matches. The 1950s and early 1960s saw the familiar decline in passenger traffic and notice was given that the passenger service would close on 30th June 1962. Since the early 1950s Ivatt 2–6–2Ts had been in use extensively on the branch and it was one of these, no 41222, which hauled the last train, a push-pull with two well-filled coaches. The days of the 'Dunstable Dasher' had come to an end.

Both Dunstable stations have been subsequently demolished. The site of the former LNWR–Dunstable North is used today by new offices for the South Bedfordshire District Council and the former GNR–Dunstable Town station site is presently vacant. At Stanbridgeford, the station building has survived as a private residence and the platform area is part of the garden. Although attractively restyled, it remains as a reminder of a 'lost line' and carries the name Stanbridgeford House.

Chapter 14

NARROW GAUGE AT PAGE'S PARK

(The Leighton Buzzard Narrow Gauge Railway)

The formal opening of the Leighton Buzzard Light Railway (LBLR) was held on the afternoon of Thursday, November 20th 1919 when a celebratory lunch was held at the town's Swan Hotel. Afterwards the directors and guests were given a ride in a specially constructed train with temporary seats fitted on four trolleys. Steam engines were not used for the occasion since they were considered 'too smoky' for passengers and the contractor's petrol engine was utilised. A good speed was maintained along the 2 ft gauge track reaching at times probably near 20 mph. The occasion went well although there were occasional unscheduled stops to allow the recovery of hats blown off in the windy weather.

Industrial sand has been used over the years for many purposes. An early application was in the making of glass although today it serves to create materials such as fibre optic cables, plastics, ceramics and so on. The greensand deposits of Leighton Buzzard have been described as 'some of the best quality in the country' with sand from one of the pits being used in the construction of the Crystal Palace. Prior to the opening of the LBLR, sand was transported from the pits to the nearby railway sidings by carts hauled by steam tractors. The roads were continually congested and they frequently required repair.

A selection of Leighton Buzzard Railway diesel locomotives at Stonehenge Works before demolition of the brickworks in the early 1980s. The scene recalls the days when sand was transported from the sand pits to the former LNWR sidings. (Christopher W Mann)

The Leighton Buzzard Railway holds a gala annually and at its 1984 event diesel no 44, a Dorman 2DL, headed a demonstration skip train at Page's Park. (Christopher W Mann)

Proposals for a railway running north eastwards from Leighton Buzzard were first made in 1892 but the LNWR showed no interest. In 1903 a line between Leighton Buzzard and Hitchin received Board of Trade approval but nothing transpired. It was not until 1914 when, following the German invasion of Belgium, supplies of imported sand were cut off and, with good quality sand in demand for munitions, production at Leighton Buzzard sub-stantially increased. A narrow-gauge rail link between the pits and the main railway sidings became a necessity although it had to wait until after the war had finished.

Following its opening, traffic increased steadily. The LBLR provided the locomotives and maintained the track while quarry owners supplied their own wagons. The line's best years came in the late 1930s and also during the Second World War when petrol for road traffic was scarce and sand once again increased in importance. In his book. *The Leighton Buzzard Light Railway*, S A Leleux wrote that during the war all sign posts, place names etc were removed to avoid helping any invading army. The company plate therefore became 'Light Railway Company Limited' and it was said that during this time at least one rail enthusiast did become confused!

After the war competition from road transport became a serious threat and this was accelerated when British Rail suffered a 17 day strike in June 1955. Many customers changed to road delivery direct from the quarry with the result that LBLR traffic dropped badly. In December 1958 the company was reorganised. The LBLR continued to own and maintain the track but the company's older locomotives were withdrawn for scrap. The six modern locomotives were sold to two quarry companies, four going to Arnold's and two to Garside's. The latter's traffic continued to decrease and five years later, in January 1963, Arnold purchased all the LBLR shares. The railway became a subsidiary with its registered office now at Arnold's office. Garside's traffic, such as it was, continued to run but tolls were paid to Arnold.

No 5 Elf 0-6-0WT at the Leighton Buzzard Light Railway, equipped with large firebox and spark arresting chimney for wood burning. The engine was built originally for the Likomba Banana Co., in Cameroon, West Africa. (Author)

It seemed the end was close when, early in 1969, British Rail announced it wanted to close the remains of the branch to Dunstable (goods traffic between Leighton Buzzard and Dunstable ceased in 1967) serving Billington Road and Grovebury sidings. With this main line link gone, the narrow-gauge line could only serve internal traffic. Meantime Arnold's applied to the County Council for permission to use lorries which would run along Shenley Hill Road, a further death-blow to the railway.

Fortunately salvation was already to hand in the name of the Iron Horse Preservation Society (IHPS) which had formed in 1967. The original plan of the IHPS had been to create an American-style railroad (plus the use of appropriate terminology) but, as time passed, members unanimously agreed that the title Leighton Buzzard Narrow Gauge Railway Society Limited (its present one) did more to provide an identity and location. It is, however, worth recording that the earlier efforts of the IHPS, such as locomotive restoration and rolling stock construction, did much to make the present society what it is today. Yet it seems the days of the Iron Horse are not totally forgotten. An item in the Society's Rule Book amusingly refers to 'the study of environmental ferroequinology and industrial archaeology . . .'

Track used by the society today covers much of the original line, comprising a stretch of almost three miles. Trains operate from Page's Park station, formerly the location of the exchange sidings, travelling past a loop at Leedon and then on beyond Vandyke Road. Quarries can of course be seen along the route – the last commercial delivery of sand on the LBLR was made on 27th March 1977. Beyond Bryan's Halt the line reaches 340 f above

A train prepares to leave Page's Park, Leighton Buzzard, for its three mile run on 2 ft narrow gauge track to Stonehenge Works. The line is popular with adults and children alike. (Author)

sea level giving splendid views back across the town of Leighton Buzzard and beyond to the Chiltern hills. The present northern terminus is at Stonehenge Works, named after the former Stonehenge Brickworks, demolished to make way for a modern tile plant.

Achievements over the years have been substantial, turning what was once a freight line into a thriving tourist attraction as well as demonstrating the part played in the development of the local sand industry. Five steam locomotives have so far been restored and work continues on a sixth. These originate from various locations around the world including Spain, West Africa and even as far as India. The oldest dates back to 1877 being *Chaloner* an 0–4–0VBT believed first used at slate quarries in Wales. There are also sixteen operational diesels plus fourteen others in stages of restoration with yet another under construction from scratch! All the rolling stock, with the exception of one (an ex-RAF Dinton coach), has been built by members as well as the station building, platforms and so forth.

The Leighton Buzzard Railway is well worth a visit. In addition there are always many tasks and opportunities for any who wish to join this fully volunteer preserved railway. From its early beginnings in 1969, membership has grown steadily. Many projects are planned for the years ahead and extra help and assistance will be needed. This is a society where enthusiasm and dedication can be clearly seen – truly it has earned the title of 'England's Friendly Little Line'.

Chapter 15

A GER LINE TO BUNTINGFORD

(St Margarets to Buntingford)

When the people of Buntingford realised they were not to be served by any main line, a meeting of landowners and interested persons was held at the George and Dragon Hotel, Buntingford on 1st August 1856, to discuss the construction of a branch of their own. It was estimated such a scheme would cost around £100,000 and, following general agreement that a railway would be favourably received, a committee was formed. A line was planned to leave the Hertford branch at Ware but certain landowners objected to this so it was decided instead to form a junction at St Margarets. Despite this, the independent company retained its original name and, on 12th July 1858, the Ware, Hadham & Buntingford Railway (WH&BR) was authorised by Parliament.

The Hertford branch with intermediate stations at Rye House, Ware and St Margarets had been in existence since 1843 leaving the main Cambridge line at Broxbourne to terminate at Hertford East. It was a Northern & Eastern Railway Company branch (later GER) opened in October 1843 and, about seven miles in length, it survives today. Ware is renowned as the home of the Wickham Works from which many railcars, overseas and light railway units have originated. Much of Ware's dark, low station building is probably original although later alterations are evident. The adjacent Station Hotel and maltings are among interesting reminders of 19th century Ware with its grain, timber and agricultural activities. The terminus, Hertford East, remains a delight to visit

A passenger train hauled by ex-LNER 0-6-2T class N7/3 no 69633 awaits departure at St Margarets for Buntingford in the 1950s. The 13¼ mile branch failed, like so many, through competition from motor cars. (Lens of Sutton)

with its 1888 station plus its imposing entrance and highly decorated main building.

The first sod of the Ware, Hadham & Buntingford Railway was cut on 20th July 1859 between Buntingford and Westmill and, according to the *Hertford Mercury*, it started as 'a jolly occasion'. In his book, *The Buntingford Branch*, P Paye wrote that after the ceremony all present went to a large marquee erected in a nearby field where a cold lunch was served. Children were catered for separately receiving large amounts of plum cake and ginger beer and the navvies were supplied with beer in a smaller tent nearby. Unfortunately the good weather quickly gave way to torrential rain and gale force winds, and water was soon penetrating the large marquee soaking tables, chairs and occupants alike. Some found shelter in the smaller tent but others were not so lucky.

It was to be a further five years before the line was completed, during which time another Act was required for an extension of time. There were financial problems during construction with the result that the Eastern Counties Railways (which formed part of the GER from 1862) subscribed £22,000. At the same time the WH&BR entered into an agreement whereby the ECR would be responsible for working, management, repair and maintenance of the line. Further problems along the 13¾ mile branch were to follow. A bridge at Braughing failed even before opening and, in addition, heavy compensation had to be paid to landowners along the route. Had the ECR not intervened, the line could well have failed before it began.

The branch opened eventually on 3rd July 1863 and a splendid banquet was held at Buntingford to celebrate the event. On the following day the *Hertford Mercury* reported, 'Buntingford was early astir yesterday morning and a great number of persons were seen wending their way to the station, anxiously awaiting the hour of departure of the first train'. Stations were decorated with flowers and banners and church bells rang at intervals. All the village schools were closed for the day and by the evening many more local folk made their way to the railway. At Hadham nearly two hundred passengers booked tickets to travel on the last train of the day, the 8.45 pm from St Margarets.

Intermediate stations were mostly wooden structures to begin with, at Mardock, Widford, Hadham, Standon, Braughing and Westmill. The line was single with passing loops and initially there were four trains each way daily with two on Sundays. The time for the journey from St Margarets to Buntingford was around 50 minutes but after the first few weeks this improved to 40 minutes. During the first half-year almost 30,000 passengers travelled the line but goods traffic was considered disappointing. This was largely due to the fact that initially there were no goods sheds or sidings!

As time passed, relations between the independent company and the newly-formed GER worsened. The WH&BR was dissatisfied with the facilities offered by the GER and the GER considered its

The former GER Ware station on the line from Broxbourne to Hertford East. It was originally planned that the Buntingford branch would leave the Hertford line at Ware but certain landowners objected and the proposal was dropped and St Margarets chosen instead. (Lens of Sutton)

Ware station in May 1991, although updated, still resembles its former structure. The Hertford East branch, which opened in 1843, is today served by a basic half-hourly service well patronised by commuters. (Author)

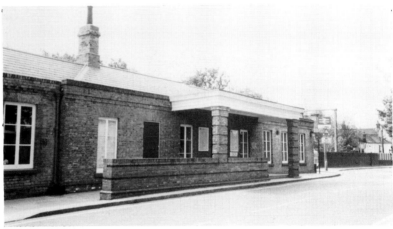

share of receipts inadequate to pay for the cost of working the line. In consequence, the GER purchased the line on 1st September 1868, just five years after the branch had opened. Problems followed and there was a derailment at Buntingford. At Westmill, a bridge constructed by an Ely contractor rotted because it had been built with low-grade timber. Track improvements were carried out and certain stations were rebuilt after which time conditions steadily improved. Freight traffic also improved with two trains daily, one to and from Broxbourne and the other to and from Hertford.

Fame came to the Buntingford branch on 13th May 1882 when the Duke and Duchess of Connaught visited Layston House, the home of their equerry and lady in waiting, Lt Col and Lady Adela Larking. A special coach was attached to the 4.55 pm train from Liverpool Street to St Margarets where it was shunted onto a branch train. On arrival at Buntingford it was greeted by over 500 onlookers and a triumphal arch of evergreens and flowers topped by a Union Jack was erected outside the Railway Hotel for the event. After a two-day stay, the couple returned by train to Liverpool Street.

Hertford East station, built in 1888, seen here in the 1970s with its imposing entrance and highly decorated building. (Lens of Sutton)

Hertford East station has changed little today. The line to the terminus was electrified as part of the North London scheme. The branch joins the main Cambridge line at Broxbourne junction. (Author)

During 1890 Braughing station, because of its remoteness, was broken into on no less than six occasions. The burglar was never caught but he certainly showed considerable audacity. Having gained entry to the booking office, he placed a lighted candle in the small window to examine the contents of the office at his leisure. He ripped open parcels and, on one occasion, stole the station master's waistcoat, coat and gold pencil case. On another occasion he made off along the line, forced an entry into a platelayer's hut and lit a fire to cook a supper of fish stolen from a parcel!

In the summer of 1901, the first through service began when the last train of the day from Buntingford ran to Liverpool Street. By 1914 there were eleven passenger trains daily although goods traffic was less encouraging. There was residential growth along the branch and from 1922 there were a number of through-coach peak-hour workings from Liverpool Street but competition from road transport was on the increase. On 1st January 1923 the Great Eastern Railway, the Great Northern Railway and the Great Central Railway and others combined to form the London & North Eastern Railway (LNER) and various economies followed. Matters worsened on 26th January 1924 when a seven day rail strike lost the line many passengers who left the trains never to return.

During the 1939–1945 war the branch acquired an additional role when it carried war supplies to and from an ordnance depot at Buntingford. Because of the importance of the traffic, bridges were frequently guarded by members of the Home Guard. Passenger services were not badly affected and during the early part of the war trains brought evacuees from London's East End, many seeing the countryside for the first time in their lives. The branch was fortunate as far as air raids were concerned, suffering only one major incident when a stray V1 flying bomb exploded near the line at Hadham. Train services were suspended for two days as a result.

After the war freight traffic declined, particularly the movement of livestock during 1950 following a serious outbreak of foot and mouth disease in the Buntingford and Standon areas. The 1950s also saw a further decline in passenger traffic as private cars began to dominate. In 1959 single diesel multiple units were introduced but by the following year many off-peak trains were cancelled. Many commuters preferred to motor to a main line rather than lose time changing at St Margarets. Towards the end of its life, the branch was used for testing prototype rail vehicles intended for export. Also a number of films were made. One of these was at Hadham which adopted the name 'Upper Fringly' in the film *Postman's Knock* featuring the locomotive J15 0–6–0 no 65460.

As passenger traffic declined, so an inevitable closure date was announced. Protests were made and public meetings were held but all was in vain. Passenger closure followed from 16th November 1964 with the last down train, comprising Rolls Royce/Derby railcars E51154/E59449/E50988, leaving St Margarets' bay platform at 9.45 pm on Saturday, 14th November. The driver was R F Hopkins and the guard W Broad. At Buntingford the train was packed for the return journey which proved to be a noisy one. Detonators exploded, the crowds cheered, the railcar gave a fanfare on its two tone horn and pulled out to the strains of 'Auld Lang Syne' and 'Wish me luck as you wave me goodbye'.

The branch, which has often been described as one of the most attractive in the Home Counties, had come to an end after over a century of service. Freight services continued for a time but on 20th September 1965 these also ceased. The former terminus at Buntingford can be found today behind the Railway Inn on the old A10 which passed through the town. It has become an office and engineering works while the platform side of the building has been lost to a housing development. Some sections of the branch trackbed have survived as footpaths but other sections have been lost following roadworks on the A10. The motorcar had indeed won the day.

Chapter 16

A MIDLAND LINE THROUGH BEDFORD

(Hitchin to Bedford and Bedford to Northampton)

Hitchin to Bedford

When a railway line was built between Hitchin and Bedford, large numbers of navvies were engaged to carry out the work. This caused considerable aggravation in the various villages along the route where the navvies' language and conduct upset the local folk and, in an effort to overcome the problem, several scripture readers were employed at 200 guineas (£210) annually to 'damp down the verbal enthusiasm'. The navvies too were irritated because of the absence of any convenient public house between Shefford and Cardington. To overcome this a private house near the line in the hamlet of Ireland was converted to become known as the Black Horse.

Application for consent to build a line from Leicester (Wigston junction) to Bedford, with an extension to Hitchin, was first submitted by the Midland Railway in 1847 but a downturn in the country's economy made the company pull back from such a new and costly project. In the early 1850s the landowners of Bedfordshire pressed the Midland to reconsider such a proposal, with the result that the application was resubmitted and on 4th August 1853 it received Parliamentary approval. The 16¼ mile double-track stretch from Hitchin to Bedford, today no longer in existence, was part of this line.

Raising capital to finance the railway was not easy since the country's economy was unsettled and the Crimean war (1853–

Hitchin station, c1910, on the main GNR route from King's Cross to Peterborough. The footbridge across the tracks was removed pre-1914. (Lens of Sutton)

1856) was threatening. Work eventually began late in 1853 but progress was slow and it became clear that a completion date set for October 1856 could not be met. Old Warden Tunnel was finished on time but only after numerous accidents, some fatal. Work on stations at Henlow, Shefford, Southill and Cardington was delayed because of a brick shortage and at Hitchin there was a dispute with the Great Northern Railway (GNR) where lines met. Because of a disagreement over valuation of a parcel of land, the Midland had to abandon a proposed junction at Arlesey and instead run alongside GNR tracks for three miles into Hitchin.

Eventually the great day arrived with a formal opening arranged for 7th May 1857. The *Bedfordshire Times* stated 'The opening of the Leicester & Hitchin Railway took place under circumstances that will be long remembered by the inhabitants of Bedford. Shops were closed, streamers waved from buildings and crowds flocked to the station to secure their places several hours before departure was due . . . at a few minutes past nine a whistle sounded, the band occupying the front carriage struck up a merry tune and the train, numbering thirty-three carriages, started slowly on its journey . . . each side of the line was thickly studded with human beings waving their handkerchiefs . . .'. When the train arrived at Leicester passengers alighted in good humour but unfortunately the railway company had forgotten to tell the inhabitants of Leicester about the new railway and the town was more than taken aback when it was 'invaded' by several thousand Bedford folk!

Initially there were four passenger trains each way on weekdays with freight services commencing some six months later. The fare from Hitchin to Leicester was 4/– (20p), second class 2/– (10p) and third class 1/– (5p). The Midland Railway claimed that it had become a London service although passengers had to change to GNR trains at Hitchin. In February 1858 the GNR allowed through Midland trains to King's Cross but charged a levy of £60,000 annually for the privilege. Meantime Midland trains were

When staff were plentiful at Hitchin GNR c1910. The canopy has long since been removed but the basic buildings remain the same. (Lens of Sutton)

having to use the LNWR station at Bedford since plans for a joint station had not materialised. It was not until February 1859 that the Midland opened its own station on Freemen's Common, nearer to the town centre.

Traffic continued at a reasonable level with market days in Hitchin and Bedford important to the local folk. On Sundays, two trains ran each way and in the summer these were popular for day trips. During the week, commuters and schoolchildren used the trains and many purchased season tickets so they could travel home for lunch. It is recorded that, on a bleak January day in 1867, Charles Dickens alighted at Bedford after a particularly rough ride from Leicester to continue his journey to London via Hitchin by a stopping train. He claimed he needed a rest from, as he put it, 'the reckless fury of the driving'.

In 1868 the Hitchin–Bedford line lost its main-line status when the Midland opened its own line from Bedford to London. The situation had been forced by earlier problems with the GNR which objected to the number of Midland trains using its King's Cross

Southill, an intermediary station on the Midland line from Hitchin to Bedford which opened in May 1857. In its time the station boasted sidings and a cattle pen. (Lens of Sutton)

Southill station closed to all traffic on 1st January 1962. Today it has become a tastefully converted private residence with an attractive garden. (Author)

sidings. In 1862 matters came to a head when the GNR summarily evicted Midland trains and the Midland saw its only future was to build an independent route. Parliamentary approval was granted in 1863 and a line via Luton and St Albans was built, reaching Moorgate Street on 13th July 1868 and St Pancras on 1st October. By 1880 the amount of traffic justified quadrupling of the track. Meantime the Hitchin–Bedford passenger services had been reduced to a shuttle service.

Plowman's Siding, between Henlow and Shefford, opened in December 1893 to accommodate wagons bringing London's household rubbish. When emptied, the wagons were filled with bricks and returned. As passenger traffic declined, so the line was converted to single except between Southill and Shefford. During the First World War a halt, Cardington Workmen's Platform, opened where in later years numerous sidings served an RAF camp. There was further activity at Cardington in the early 1920s when the then Labour Government approved the construction of two large airships for Empire communication, the R100 and the R101. Two vast sheds were required to house them and Cardington was to prove an ideal site.

The original shed was built by Short Bros during 1916/17 as part of a contract to build rigid airships for the Admiralty to support the war effort. The group of nearby houses, built to house employees, became known as 'Shortstown' – a name it still holds today. The first rigid airship was the R31 which flew just before the end of the war but following the Armistice, the airship programme was wound down although Cardington remained an active base. Interest was revived when the R100 arrived in December 1929 from Howden in Yorkshire where it had been built and it successfully flew the Atlantic both ways the following year. To house it, the original shed had to be re-erected and to assist with this a rail line was laid from the nearby station. A second shed to match the first was dismantled and transported to Cardington from its original location at Pulham in Norfolk during the winter of 1928/29.

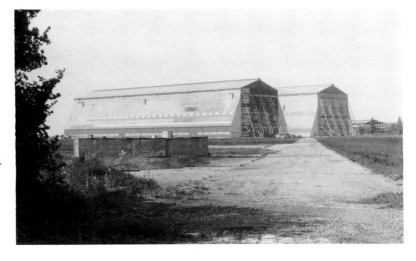

Not far from the former Cardington station, these massive airsheds still exist. It was in one of these that the ill-fated R101 was housed, the airship which crashed dramatically in France in October 1930. (Author)

Ex-Midland Railway class 2F 0-6-0 no 3707 (built 1901 to a design of S W Johnson) at Bedford on 10th August 1935. (D K Jones)

The R101 first flew in September 1929, three years behind schedule, and it proved to be overweight. To overcome this it was lengthened and an extra gas cell installed. After just one test flight, it left for India (without proper testing) and crashed dramatically 7½ hours into the flight near Allone in France. Following the crash, the R100 was broken up and the airship programme terminated. Since that time the sheds have been used in many ways including the development of barrage balloons during the Second World War. One of the sheds has for many years been a centre for fire research although in more recent years the other returned to its original role housing 'Skyships' of Airship Industries. This company went out of business in 1990 and the shed currently houses motor cars. Yet the past is not forgotten thanks to FOCAS (Friends of Cardington Airship Station) which also regularly produces a fascinating journal called *Dirigible*.

When buses came to the area in the 1920s the railway began a slow decline from which it did not recover. Activity renewed somewhat when RAF camps were established in the area during the Second World War and platforms at Henlow (renamed Henlow Camp in 1933) were extended to cope with special troop trains. By the 1950s trains comprised one carriage only and it was clear that the end was in sight. The introduction of a diesel service in 1960 did little to encourage traffic and the line closed as from 1st January 1962.

As the last train from Bedford to Hitchin prepared to pull out of Midland Road station, railway enthusiasts were there in force. Before it left, there was a cheer as Richard Lentam of the Biggleswade & District Model Railway Society placed a wreath on locomotive 2–6–2T no 84005 and, exactly on time, driver Wilf Johnson eased the train away from the platform. Before the line was finally lifted, it had one last claim to fame when a film company making *Those Magnificent Men in their Flying Machines* acquired the disused line and the tunnel. The film depicted an air race in the early days of aviation and at one point Terry Thomas's aircraft

Olney station on the line from Bedford to Northampton which closed to passengers on 5th March 1962. In its heyday, the stationmaster was very proud of the chrysanthemums grown in the station garden. (Lens of Sutton)

crashed onto a train. The locomotive was ex-Highland Railway no 103 plus a set of coaches disguised to appear as a French train.

Anyone visiting the area today can find many recollections of the past. One of these is the station building at Southill which has been tastefully converted into a private residence. The ticket window is still there but looking through to show a kitchen rather than a ticket office. The platform area, sidings and cattle pen have become a garden to be proud of. Not far from Southill station and hidden among trees is an obelisk erected in 1864 as a memorial to William Henry Whitbread as a tribute to his 'zeal and energy in promoting railways in the county'. At Old Warden the tunnel can still be found, now a nature reserve in the safe keeping of the Beds and Hunts Wildlife Trust.

Cardington station buildings have survived but the area is lost in scrap metal. Many of the houses in the village date back to the 17th century and ghost stories are quite common. It is said that several of the properties are haunted by members of the ill-fated R101 airship crew who have come back to look for their loved ones. . . .

Bedford to Northampton

The first attempt to build a railway between Bedford and Northampton was made in 1845 by a company known as the 'Northampton, Bedford & Cambridge Railway'. It was planned to reach Bedford at the station today known as St John's with a projected line to Cambridge to follow. The plan failed to materialise and the company collapsed with shareholders having some of their investment refunded. The route was surveyed again in 1864 but, according to the *Bedfordshire Mercury*, this scheme was dropped because of huge demands made by the owners of property. It was finally an Act obtained in 1865 that gave the go-ahead but, due to delays in obtaining finance plus the obtaining of a satisfactory contractor, further Acts had to be obtained in 1866 and 1867 to provide an extension of time.

Turvey station c1910. Passenger traffic was light since this was a very rural area with the station situated over a mile from Turvey village. There were five trains each way on weekdays but never any Sunday services. (Lens of Sutton)

Today at Turvey the platforms have gone but the attractive stone building remains to serve as an office to a company of agricultural merchants. (Author)

The line was promoted by Colonel Higgins of Turvey and William Henry Whitbread, the latter being responsible for many railways in Bedfordshire. His death in 1867 was an untimely blow to the branch's fortunes since his skill and drive had contributed a great deal. Work on the line suffered in consequence and it was not until 1870 that construction picked up again at a satisfactory rate. In March 1872 it was announced that completion was further delayed by heavy rains causing damage to cuttings and embankments. The terrain also caused problems. Between Bedford and Northampton there is a plateau of high ground approximately 350 ft above sea level known at Yardley Chase and this involved steep gradients. In the days to come, enginemen on the branch referred to a trip as 'going over the Alps'.

The 21-mile line eventually opened on 10th June 1872 but due to the death of the Duke of Bedford it was considered correct to delay the celebrations until later in the month. When they took place on 26th July, a grand banquet was held in Bedford's Assembly Rooms and many dignitaries were present. In a speech, the chairman, Colonel Higgins, included a welcome for the many distinguished people from Northampton and, replying, the High Sheriff of Northampton spoke of the days when a horse-drawn journey from Bedford to Northampton took three hours.

The branch left the Midland line north of Bedford at Oakley junction and there were intermediate stations at Turvey, Olney and Piddington. Like many rural stations two of them were some distance from the locality they claimed to serve. Turvey station with its attractive stone building was over a mile from its village although Olney, also in stone, was well placed in the town. Piddington was brick-built but very isolated and hard to find along a narrow country lane with its village 2½ miles away. The branch ended at St John's Street in the middle of Northampton.

Initially there were five trains each way on weekdays but there was never any Sunday service. In January 1881 there was a severe blizzard and the evening train to Bedford became stuck in a snowdrift which had also brought down telegraph poles. F G Cockman wrote in the *Bedfordshire Magazine* that devotion to duty took place that night, but it was not just confined to the railway staff. Mrs Rose Sargeant, the Turvey postmistress, had taken the postbag to the station as usual that evening. She stayed there all night waiting in vain for the train to arrive and would not part with the bag until the next morning.

In 1923 the Midland Railway became part of the London, Midland & Scottish Railway (LMS) and in July 1939 it was decided to cut expenses by closing Northampton's St John's Street station. Trains were switched to the Castle station via Harding-stone junction. By this time the number of passengers was declining although specials were seen along the branch when there was horse-racing at Towcester. During the 1939–1945 war the line regained importance with well-packed trains once again. Piddington station also became busier when an Army depot opened nearby.

After the war, competition from motor transport increased and efforts were made to attract passengers. For a time diesel railcars took over from steam but they frequently broke down and steam trains were brought back. But it was too late since local folk were finding other ways to travel. Towards its end, the branch developed a very rural flavour. Track gangs snared rabbits in Ravenstone Wood and train drivers left orders sometimes leaving coal in payment. At Olney the stationmaster was proud of his chrysanthemums in the station garden and often used paper bags to protect them from the rain. They became known as 'the paper bag harvest'.

The last train hauled by an Ivatt 2-6-2T ran on 3rd March 1962, crammed with passengers. There were exploding detonators on the track and the usual wreaths were placed on the engine. Notices stuck on the windows of the two-coach push-pull read, 'Bedford–Northampton. Killed by the internal combustion engine. Farewell. RIP'. Ninety years of faithful service had come to an end.

Chapter 17

TOWARDS CAMBRIDGE

(Bedford to Sandy and Potton)

Visit the parish church in Sandy and it is possible to find a monument commemorating the life of Captain William Peel, VC, the third son of Sir Robert Peel. Captain Peel was an extraordinary man for in his 34 years he sailed much of the world in the navy, saw service in Syria, China, America, the Crimea and India and explored the African interior. He was one of the early recipients of the Victoria Cross and his daring feats included on one occasion throwing a live shell with the fuse still burning from the parapet of his battery in the Crimea back at the Russians. The end of the Crimean War meant a return to England but for Captain Peel this presented a further challenge for his love of action – so he built a railway.

He had already purchased some 1,400 acres of land in 1852 in anticipation and because he now owned the land no Act of Parliament was necessary. He also purchased a locomotive for £800 (built by George England & Co of Hatcham ironworks). In 1857 Captain Peel set sail for service in China in his frigate *Shannon* but at Singapore his ship was diverted to Calcutta to deal with a mutiny where he again distinguished himself. It was in India that he met his untimely end for he died on April 22nd 1858 during an epidemic of smallpox. Sadly he never lived to see his railway completed.

The Sandy & Potton Railway was initially intended for goods traffic only and on 23rd June 1857, the grand opening ceremony was performed by Lady Peel, Captain Peel's mother. At the occasion she named the engine *Shannon* after the frigate her son had commanded. Both towns were 'agog with excitement and gay with decorations'. Banners and evergreens were everywhere and a triumphal arch was built carrying slogans such as 'Captain William Peel and Progress', 'Perseverance and Industry will join Potton and Cambridge' and, recalling the incident in the Crimea, 'In Remembrance of the Live Shell, October 18th, 1854'. A giant marquee, 120 ft by 30 ft, was erected seating over 400 people to lunch at a cost of 2/6d (12½p) each to include a pint of beer. The 3½ mile single-track line ran from Potton to Sandy with one cutting and a curve (near Caesar's Camp) to form a junction with the Great Northern Railway (GNR) on the Biggleswade side of Sandy.

At first rolling stock consisted of *Shannon* and another tank engine, a brake van, two wagons and a trolley. On 9th November 1857 the line opened to passenger traffic with coaches hired from the GNR. Signalling consisted of 'waving a red flag when a would-be passenger from one of the farmhouses passed along the route wished to embark'. Although agricultural traffic proved to be busy,

Northbound GNR 4-4-2 locomotive no 1416 with passenger train at Sandy station c1910. This class 251 locomotive, designed by H G Ivatt, was built about 1906 and became an LNER class C1. (Lens of Sutton)

Sandy station in the 1960s not long before closure of the Bedford to Cambridge branch which used the far platform in this picture. Quadrupling of the main GNR line has today obliterated the branch station. (Lens of Sutton)

passenger traffic was never outstanding, principally because the company failed to produce an extension towards Cambridge. Instead the railway was purchased in 1862 by the Bedford & Cambridge Railway (B&CR) for £20,000 to include *Shannon*. The locomotive was then resold to the contractor, Joseph Firbank, for use in constructing the new line.

At Potton the B&CR track swung northwards with a station built close to the Red Lion Inn. This made the original Sandy & Potton Railway terminus and locomotive shed (which housed *Shannon*) become redundant with the engine house later becoming a vegetable store. The B&CR opened on 6th August 1860 and was worked by the LNWR from the outset but was absorbed by the LNWR in 1865 when finance became difficult. It was initially single track but as traffic grew the line was doubled between Sandy and Cambridge. The section between Bedford and Sandy remained single to avoid the expense of rebuilding river bridges.

The B&CR at Bedford (renamed Bedford St Johns in 1924)

Potton station looking towards Gamlingay and Cambridge showing some of the intricate cast ironwork in the brackets. The station closed to goods traffic on 1st January 1966 and to passenger traffic on 1st January 1968. (Lens of Sutton)

started at an end-on junction with the LNWR branch from Bletchley. Through traffic was later possible, but no such arrangement followed to produce a joint station with the Midland Railway branch from Hitchin to Leicester. Strenuous efforts, supported by the Mayor of Bedford, were made in vain and passengers justifiably complained about having to walk across the town in all weathers to change trains. Between Bedford and Potton there were intermediate stations at Blunham and Sandy. Initially there were eight trains each way daily from Bedford to Cambridge with one each way on Sundays. LNWR four wheel coaches were used with six wheel stock being introduced around 1880.

Willington station opened on 1st May 1903. The villagers had petitioned for a station when the line opened but without success, although a siding was installed in September 1896 mainly for agricultural goods. Immediately prior to the station's opening, the *Bedford Times* reported, 'At first trains will not stop except when required. Persons wishing to alight must give notice at the preceding station, and when passengers wish to join the train it will be stopped by signal'. Blunham station, a substantial building of brick construction, had two platforms plus sidings and, in addition, a longer siding leading to a linseed oil mill on the banks of the river Ivel. Between Blunham and Sandy where the A1 crossed the track, the LMSR opened a small halt in 1938 to encourage local traffic but it lasted only two years. There was no station building and tickets had to be purchased at a nearby garage.

At Sandy the line from Bedford crossed the GNR line from Hitchin to Peterborough and the two companies shared the same station site. Before reaching Sandy and after crossing the GNR tracks, B&CR trains curved to run down a gradient to the platform. Until 1917 Sandy had two station-masters although an exchange siding existed between the two companies which jointly handled many tons of agricultural produce each week. Travellers on the Bedford line could enjoy their brief stop. Not only was Sandy station well known for its attractive flowerbeds and shrubs but in later years there could be an occasional glimpse of the *Flying Scotsman* thundering past on its journey between King's Cross and Edinburgh.

Potton, situated on the borders of Bedfordshire and Cambridgeshire, can boast a long established and lively community. It has been described as an 'outstanding conservation area of architectural and historic interest'. During its life it has suffered more than once from serious fires. Fifty houses had to be rebuilt after their destruction in 1783 and there were further bad fires in 1870 and 1878 after which occasions it was decided to form a properly organised fire brigade. Prior to the arrival of the railways, transport was sparse. In the early 1830s, a coach left the Green Man for London each week and in 1847 a weekly omnibus left The Swan for the Smithfield market in London. It was ten years later in 1857 that Captain Peel's privately constructed Potton to Sandy railway was built.

Happily for posterity the station buildings and platforms at Potton have been preserved, although as a strictly private residence. There is much to recall the past – even the ventilation grilles in the building carry the letters BCR in script – a reminder of the Bedford and Cambridge Railway. (Author)

The subsequent Potton B&CR station was substantially built with a cast-iron canopy supported by stanchions carrying intricate cast-ironwork on the 'up' platform. During its earlier days large quantities of agricultural goods, such as potatoes and onions, left the area while considerable consignments of manure came in for the farmers. Much of this came from stables in London with further quantities coming from London Zoo. In his book *Oxford to Cambridge*, volume two, Bill Simpson wrote that a cargo quite unique to the area was a fertilizer called 'coprolites' (thought to be fossilized faeces of Mesozoic reptiles) found in large quantities near the surface on sites between Sandy and Potton. Such was the demand for the commodity that orders came from as far away as

Newcastle-upon-Tyne. One order from Wolverhampton called for 1,500 tons at 9/2d (46p) per ton.

0-4-0WT Wantage no 5, built 1857, seen here at the Wantage Tramway. This locomotive at one time served the Sandy & Potton Railway known as Shannon. It can be found today as a stationary exhibit at Didcot Railway Centre. (Lens of Sutton)

In December 1914, not long after the outbreak of the First World War, the Bedford to Cambridge line was for a time requisitioned for heavy military traffic. Normal services were suspended while a succession of troop trains covered the line at intervals of twenty minutes. At Cambridge they continued their journeys on Great Eastern tracks enabling a large proportion of Kitchener's Army to eventually reach France. In January 1923 the line became part of the London, Midland & Scottish Railway (LMS) under the 1921 Amalgamation of Railways Act. When the Second World War came in 1939 the line once again saw active service. One role during hostilities was the operation of petrol trains to an RAF petrol supply depot not far from Sandy. Supplies were sent to airfields throughout East Anglia and for the three month period following D-Day over 600 trains left Sandy at the rate of seven a day.

The first suggestion that the line might close came in May 1959 and immediately there was strong local opposition. In the face of this BR introduced new diesel multiple units to encourage traffic and for a time matters improved. In March 1963 the Beeching Plan was published but it was not until the end of the year that BR announced final closure would be in February 1964. Opposition again proved successful with a suspension obtained pending a public enquiry with the East Anglia & East Midland Transport Users' Consultative Committee. At a meeting held in July 1964 the local authorities strongly pointed out that loss of the service would cause great hardship to the community but BR argued that the line was losing almost £100,000 annually. Despite difficulties in arranging replacement bus services, complete closure came on 1st January 1968 with Bedford St Johns becoming the terminus for the trains from Bletchley. This latter line came close to closure on several occasions even to the point that more than once 'Withdrawal of Railway Passenger Services' notices were posted. Despite such attempts the line remains open today with the possibility that it might assume a greater role at some future date (chapter 4).

In the wake of closure of the Bedford to Cambridge line came a proposal that a section of the line might be preserved. A public meeting was held and the Sandy & Potton Steam Railway Society was formed. The interest was in a 5¼ mile stretch towards Cambridge between Potton and Gamlingay but, despite support from Sandy UDC, lack of funds plus the expense of repairing a bridge over the line at Potton which had become unsafe made the project impractical. Plans were finally frustrated when the track was removed from July 1969 and the society was wound up.

The most interesting relic of the line today can be found at Potton where the station buildings and platforms have survived. On the platform the stanchions with their elegant ironwork continue to support the canopy and the building (now a strictly private residence) carries recollections of the past. The ticket office with its hatch is still there and a BR notice board gives details from the past. Numerous further relics add to the superb realism even to the small ventilation grilles around the building which carry the letters BCR in script letters.

A further relic from the past is the locomotive *Shannon*. In 1863 this gallant little engine from the Sandy & Potton Railway went to Crewe for fifteen year's shunting service to be sold in 1878 to the Wantage Tramway Company. Following final closure of the tramway in 1945, *Shannon* found numerous further locations and today it stands with pride as a stationary exhibit at the Didcot Railway Centre.

CONCLUSION

The decline of many branches began in the 1920s. Buses were able to offer a more flexible service than the trains and road haulage was on the increase. In addition the private motor car was beginning to make its presence felt. After nationalisation in 1948, the railways, still recovering from the demands of war service, were slow to meet any competition and were losing ground. Reduced revenue was leading to increased economies and then closures, with the entire pattern of inland transport gradually changing.

An early casualty was the Wolverton & Stony Stratford Tramway which closed in May 1926. Serious competition first came in 1914 when motor buses from Bedford extended their service to Stony Stratford and by the end of the First World War the condition of the trams was described as 'little more than derelict'. The system struggled on, but on 4th May 1926, during the General Strike, services were suspended never to be resumed.

Further closures came when the London Passenger Transport Board decided to discontinue suburban services beyond Aylesbury and in consequence two outposts from the Metropolitan Railway days were closed. The Brill branch (formerly the Wotton Tramway) came to an end on 30th November 1935 and, on 6th July 1936, passenger traffic from Quainton Road to Verney Junction ceased when the line was reduced to single track and used for goods traffic only. The previously-enjoyed building expansion had slowed down and, when the 1939–1945 war came, the 'Metro-dream' was at an end.

Another casualty came soon after the war ended. The 'Nicky' line from Hemel Hempstead to Harpenden survived the war but passenger services were withdrawn in June 1947 during a coal crisis. Freight struggled on for a time but by the mid-1960s this also ceased. Closures accelerated during the early 1950s as competition increased and the motor car was taking over. Lines that years ago had bustled with traffic such as the Hatfield to St Albans Abbey line or the branches to Aylesbury, Hertford or Rickmansworth all succumbed. In Buckinghamshire, the former GWR branch from Princes Risborough which crossed the border to Watlington in Oxfordshire saw its last passenger train in June 1957 after 85 years of faithful service with closure from 1st July 1957.

In March 1963 proposals were made in a report which became popularly known as the 'Beeching Plan'. Basically the idea was to keep lines considered suitable to rail traffic and give up the remainder. It was claimed that one third of the rail system in Britain carried only 1% of the total traffic!

Further drastic cuts inevitably followed and many more lines disappeared. Closures – once a trickle – had become a torrent. Where once existed branches, some linking major routes across the region, soon only the original trunk routes remained. A number of isolated branches survived but their future can only be uncertain.

However, the railway's past has not been forgotten. At Quainton Road steam lives on where one can find a fascinating collection of locomotives and rolling stock. Not only the days of the Metropolitan Railway are recalled but also the time when Sir Edward Watkin had a vision of through trains from the Midlands to the South Coast and beyond to Paris. At Leighton Buzzard a narrow-gauge railway brings back memories of the time when industrial sand was transported by wagons to sidings on the branch line to Dunstable. Today at Page's Park, the line has become a strong tourist attraction.

What of the future for the Chilterns area? Despite British Rail's current and extensive modernisation programmes, is it possible that the ever-increasing fares will push many of the commuters and travellers off the trains that still remain? Although passenger traffic may suffer, there appears hope that certain freight traffic may return if the proposed Euro-Freighter can replace the juggernaut on our already overcrowded roads. With the European Open Market coming in 1992 and the Channel Tunnel planned to open in 1993, both these events are likely to have a considerable impact on the railways and the movement of goods in particular.

An exciting prospect for the future is the possibility of a £1.5 billion rail tunnel from Paddington to Liverpool Street that would link Buckinghamshire and Berkshire in the west with Essex in the east. Plans for such a line were announced in July 1991 by London Underground and Network Southeast with a proposed opening date in 1999. Such a link would mean that trains from Reading, Aylesbury and Amersham could run through the seven mile proposed tunnel to Shenfield, via Stratford and Romford without a need for passengers to change. It is hoped that a journey from Amersham to Tottenham Court Road will take 28 minutes compared with the present 50 minutes. A Bill is expected to be presented to Parliament in November 1991 and building could commence in 1994.

A further interesting development for the Chilterns area is the possibility that light railway schemes might return to relieve the increasingly crowded roads. The current successes of the Docklands Light Railway and the Tyne and Wear Metro have brought about numerous applications to build new systems elsewhere, including the Greater Manchester Rapid Transit, the Midland Metro and many others. There have been numerous proposals over the surviving single track between Luton and Dunstable, one of these being a tramway system giving an 11-station line to include Luton Airport. On the airport section existing highways would be used.

At Milton Keynes, the new town founded in 1967, the council has commissioned a feasibility study into the possibility of a rapid transit system linking the town centre with Bletchley, Newport Pagnell, Wolverton and Stony Stratford. Where housing near the town centre might make this impractical, then a partially elevated system may be considered.

Can it really be that such light railways may make a come-back along once-axed lines or trackbeds? These are certainly exciting times for railways in the Chilterns area. Can we hope for regular passenger services to return between Bicester and Bletchley and that Verney Junction may once again spring back into life? Is it possible that the former GCR line to Rugby will ever re-open to provide a fast route to the Midlands when the Channel Tunnel is built? How Sir Edward Watkin would have been fascinated by such ideas.

OPENING AND FINAL CLOSURE DATES OF LINES TO REGULAR PASSENGER TRAFFIC

Line	Opened	Final Closure
Cheddington/Aylesbury	10 June 1839	2 Feb 1953
Dunstable/Leighton Buzzard	1 June 1848	26 April 1965
Banbury (Merton Street)/Buckingham	1 May 1850	2 Jan 1961
Buckingham/Verney Junction	1 May 1850	7 Sept 1964
Bletchley/Verney Jct	1 May 1850	1 Jan 1968
Verney Jct/Islip	1 Oct 1850	1 Jan 1968
Islip/Oxford	20 May 1851	1 Jan 1968
Bourne End/High Wycombe	1 Aug 1854	2 May 1970
Hitchin/Bedford	8 May 1857	1 Jan 1962
Sandy/Potton	9 Nov 1857	1 Jan 1968*[1]
Hertford/Hatfield	1 March 1858	18 June 1951
Luton/Dunstable	3 May 1858	26 April 1965
Hatfield/Luton	1 Sept 1860	26 April 1965
Bedford/Sandy/Cambridge	7 July 1862	1 Jan 1968
Princes Risborough/Thame	1 Aug 1862	7 Jan 1963
Watford/Rickmansworth	1 Oct 1862	3 March 1952
St Margarets/Buntingford	3 July 1863	16 Nov 1964
Thame/Oxford	24 Oct 1864	7 Jan 1963
Hatfield/St Albans Abbey	16 Oct 1865	1 Oct 1951
Wolverton/Newport Pagnell	2 Sept 1867	6 Sept 1964
Aylesbury/Quainton Road	23 Sept 1868	5 Sept 1966
Quainton Road/Verney Jct	23 Sept 1868	6 July 1936
Quainton Road/Brill	April 1872	30 Nov 1935
Bedford/Northampton	10 June 1872	5 March 1962
Princes Risborough/Watlington	15 Aug 1872	1 July 1957
Hemel Hempstead/Harpenden	16 July 1877	16 June 1947
Wolverton/Stony Stratford	27 May 1887	4 May 1926
Quainton Road/Brackley Central/Rugby	15 March 1899	5 Sept 1966
Ashendon Jct/Grendon Underwood Jct	2 April 1906	7 Dec 1953

*[1]Merged with Bedford & Cambridge Railway in 1862

INDEX